S0-AAK-857

MEDIA TESTIMONIALS

Dhaval Bathia packs in quite a cerebral punch. A unique, blend of talent, insight, hardwork and sheer determination.

— The Times of India

'Dhaval Bathia is a Wizard.'

— The Gulf Today

'One of the greatest intellectuals that India has produced.'

— Jazbaat Magazine

Dhaval Bathia is simply excellent. His workshops are commendable.

— Maharashtra Times

'A Young Achiever. His seminars have received a tremendous response from the corporate world.'

— Education World Magazine

He **SWAM** with **SHARKS** for an **ICE-CREAM**

He SWAM with SHARKS for an ICE-CREAM

An inspiring story about fulfilling your dreams and achieving success

Dhaval Bathia

JAICO PUBLISHING HOUSE

Ahmedabad Bangalore Bhopal Chennai
Delhi Hyderabad Kolkata Lucknow Mumbai

Published by Jaico Publishing House
A-2 Jash Chambers, 7-A Sir Phirozshah Mehta Road
Fort, Mumbai - 400 001
jaicopub@jaicobooks.com
www.jaicobooks.com

© Dhaval Bathia

HE SWAM WITH SHARKS FOR AN ICE-CREAM
ISBN 978-81-8495-066-3

First Jaico Impression: 2010

This book is a work of fiction. All characters, incidents,
figures and other events are purely imaginary or coincidental.
Much of the data collected in the book is through third party
testimonials and neither the author nor the publisher
claim authenticity of the same.

No part of this book may be reproduced or utilized in
any form or by any means, electronic or
mechanical including photocopying, recording or by any
information storage and retrieval system,
without permission in writing from the publishers.

Printed by
Rashmi Graphics
#3, Amrutwel CHS Ltd., C.S. #50/74
Ganesh Galli, Lalbaug, Mumbai-400 012
E-mail: tiwarijp@vsnl.net

CONTENTS

CONTENTS

ACKNOWLEDGEMENTS

I would like to thank my family, friends, colleagues, clients, and publishers, without whose support and encouragement, this book would not have been possible. I dedicate this book to Raj, my nephew.

PROLOGUE

Have you ever noticed? When you are at work, bad news is conveyed to you only after you have just settled down with your first mug of coffee. It is as if destiny times it so, to counter the effects of caffeine. That day was no exception to this rule.

As soon as I had poured myself a mug of hot coffee and settled in my chair, I saw an e-mail notification flash on my screen — From: deepak.patel@omgroup.com.

A mail from the Boss? I asked myself in surprise. It was very unusual to receive a mail from him. Most of his communications were very informal. Either he would talk to us over the phone or meet us in person; in either case, one was forced to listen to his gruff voice. Meeting him was worse, as he looked a lot like Hitler. In fact, when he wasn't around, we often referred to him as 'Hitler'.

I read the e-mail. It was addressed to my colleague Abhi Thakur and myself:

To: *abhi.thakur@omgroup.com; dave.fernandes@omgroup.com*

Dear Abhi and Dave,

Both of you have been selected for a special assignment. For the next few days, you will be working with the Founder President of Om Group, Mr. Haribhai Shah.

Currently, he is involved in various rural development projects in western India.

You will receive further instructions and details once you get there.

All the best on your new assignment. Hope you get 'THE SHIFT'!

Yours sincerely,
Deepak Patel

PS: Sameer, our CEO is sure Mr. Haribhai Shah will be able to help you understand all about 'Bania Buddhi'.

I had hardly finished reading this when my phone rang. It was my colleague, Abhi.

"Dave, did you read Deepak's mail?"

"Yes, I just did."

"Man, this is shit!" he screamed. "We have been posted to some remote village."

"And during the hottest part of the year," I sulked.

"What do these guys think?" Abhi was disgusted. "I am an MBA from one of India's top B-schools and they want me to go to this cowdung place and learn from Harry Shah, that old grandfather!"

"Ssshh! Be polite, dude! He is Sameer's father. Our CEO's father. And don't forget he founded our multi-billion dollar company."

Harry Shah was how Haribhai Shah was known these days. He was the founder of Om Group, the company we worked for. Since his foreign clients couldn't pronounce 'Haribhai', they called him 'Harry', and the name stuck.

"Damn it," Abhi exploded, "we are here to do executive-level work. I am not going anywhere."

I could understand Abhi's frustration, I myself was agitated. He had earned his MBA from one of India's top B-schools, and quite obviously he expected something much better than a job in a village.

"Hey Abhi," I said, "Did you read Hitler's mail carefully? He has mentioned 'The Shift'."

"Don't say it!" he snapped, "It's getting on my nerves. Ever since I joined this company, not a single major task has been assigned to me. Everybody says that it will happen only after I get 'The Shift'."

"Yes, I know. All new recruits hear this all the time, 'Get The Shift', 'Get The Shift', 'Get The Shift'."

"But Dave, that's not all. They don't even explain what they mean!" he whined.

Abhi was right. It was obvious that new recruits felt excluded by all other employees in Om Group. It was assumed that new recruits were those who had still not got 'The Shift'. And when senior colleagues were asked to explain what the shift was about, they would reply curtly, 'The Shift cannot be explained in words. It has to be experienced!'

Damn it! It was better to remain ignorant than to ask them.

"Chillax Abhi!" I said, "Anyway, we have to go there. Might as well take the whole thing in our stride," saying so, I hung up.

I settled back in my chair and started drinking my coffee, which had by then become too cold to have any effect on my nerves. Hardly a minute had gone by when Abhi called again.

"Hey Dave, it's about Hitler's mail," he asked urgently, "Did you read it carefully?"

"What about it now?" I groaned, not looking forward to thinking about it any more.

"Did you read the last two words?"

"Wait a minute. Let me open the Inbox again."

I opened the mail and saw the last two words — 'Bania Buddhi'.

My eyes skimmed over the sentence, comprehending each word one by one — 'Sameer, our CEO is sure Mr. Haribhai Shah will be able to help you understand all about 'Bania Buddhi'.

"Bun..ee..ya Budhee," I read aloud.

"Do you understand it?" Abhi asked impatiently.

"I have never heard it before."

"Nor have I," said Abhi.

"Hey, why don't we Google it?" I suggested.

"Oh good idea!" exclaimed Abhi. "Give me a minute."

I could hear Abhi tapping away on the keyboard.

"Huh! Only one search result."

"Only one! Have you spelt it correctly?" I asked, "Even the most obscure phenomena would fetch a few dozen results on Google."

"I know. But there is only one entry for this."

"What's it?" I asked impatiently.

"Wait."

He was silent for a while. I thought of googling the words myself.

Suddenly, Abhi spoke quickly and with great excitement, "Oh boy! You got to see this! The link took me to an old interview with Dhirubhai Ambani."

"Dhirubhai Ambani? The multi-billionaire businessman?" I asked.

"Of course, Dave. There is only one Dhirubhai Ambani."

"Tell me more," I said, forgetting about my cold coffee.

"It is a rare interview with Dhirubhai, which he gave the editor of a leading business magazine, before his death."

"And what does it say?"

"Well, it says many things. But I will get to the crux of it. The interviewer asks Dhirubhai Ambani, 'How did a man like yourself, from a poor family in rural India, with no formal education and without any proper resource, become India's richest man? What is the secret? Is it your world-class approach, insistence on quality, or daring entrepreneurship? And Dhirubhai says, 'all of that, alongwith some Bania Buddhi'."

What is this 'Bania Buddhi'? I asked myself. Curiosity was something that I had never been able to control.

I was about to get an answer soon, very soon.

I

AT THE EDGE OF A NEW BEGINNING

How was it that 'Bania Buddhi', something that the legendary Dhirubhai Ambani had spoken about, had never been discussed in any business magazine? In fact, even Abhi wasn't aware of it. If it was related to the greatest Indian entrepreneur then at least B-schools should have taught it. After all, that's what B-schools were supposed to do, teach you the strategies of great entrepreneurs.

I wanted to double check the whole thing myself. I typed the words 'Bania Buddhi' in the search engine and waited.

Only one search result. Abhi was right.

The link to the old interview with Ambani had been published in June 2002, about a month before he died. The article began with a brief description of Dhirubhai's achievements:

Dhirubhai Ambani was born in Chorwad, a small village in Gujarat, India. His father was a poor school teacher and could not afford his son's higher education. So, Dhirubhai had to quit his studies after the tenth grade. He went to Aden, a small town in the Middle East, so that he could support his family. He found a job as a petrol pump attendant. He received a meager salary and lived a happy life. Years later, with strong desire to do something for his country and his people, Dhirubhai returned to India.

He started a small company by investing all his savings, which was just about Rs. 50,000 ($1,250).

And the rest as we all know is history...

Today, Dhirubhai's company, Reliance, is India's largest company and the only private company featured in the Fortune 500 list. The annual turnover of the Reliance Group is $13.2 billion. Reliance has about 4 million shareholders, the highest in the world.

The boy who worked at a petrol pump today owns a huge empire dealing in synthetic fibers, textiles, petrochemical products, oil and gas energy, life sciences, telecommunications, logistics, power and infrastructure services, and financial services.

In 1976-77, Reliance had an annual turnover of Rs 70 crore ($17.5 million). Fifteen years later, it became Rs 3,000 crore ($750 million). By the end of the century, the amount had skyrocketed to Rs 60,000 crore. In 25 years, the value of Reliance Group assets has jumped from Rs 33 crore to

33,000 crore. ($ 8.25 million) to ($ 8250 million).

Reliance contributes to 5% of India's total exports, 10% of the government's indirect tax revenues, 30% of total profits from the private sector, 10% profits from the entire corporate sector, and 7% of the total market capitalisation in India.

Ambani has been thrice adjudged one of the 50 most powerful men in Asia; FICCI awarded him the 'Indian Entrepreneur Of 20th Century' award, The Times of India poll decided he was 'Creator of Wealth of the Century'; Wharton School of Business awarded him the prestigious 'Dean's Medal'; among several other honours.

———

Phew! Was this man for real? His achievements sounded too good to be true.

I had always known that Dhirubhai Ambani was a big achiever, but these facts were not big achievements...they were Gigantic.

And yes, the article clearly mentioned Ambani crediting his success to Bania Buddhi. But, it wasn't explained.

Suddenly, what had started as just another dull morning in the office began to seem exciting. I tried to recollect the words in the e-mail...

'Sameer, our CEO is sure Mr. Haribhai Shah will be able

to help you understand all about 'Bania Buddhi'.'

Wow! This is so exciting! I said to myself. This means
Hitler is sending us on a special project to get 'The Shift'
and understand 'Bania Buddhi'.

For the first time in two weeks since I had joined the
company, my boss was giving me something worthwhile. It
felt good.

But, why choose Abhi and me for the project? There were
many others who were better qualified.

And how could Harry know Dhirubhai Ambani's business
secrets? Was there any connection between them?

Many questions remained unanswered.

The only thing I knew for certain was that there would be
at least one kind of shift. From a cosy, sophisticated office
in posh Mumbai, to some unknown village in rural India.

2

AN UNKNOWN DESTINATION

Abhi and I came from very different backgrounds. What made us get along together, was our age. Both of us were in our late twenties.

He was a typical B-school grad. About 5'6" tall, fair, bright eyes, and blessed with supernatural intelligence. He had the uncanny ability to impress anybody by using jargon and he was well-known for drawing imaginary 'demand and supply curves' by just doodling in the air each time he tried to explain a difficult concept.

I was like any other creative guy working in an ad agency. Tall, lanky, with long hair right down to my shoulder, a goatee, and a pierced ear. Formal clothes made me feel uncomfortable. I preferred my Metallica or Guns-n-Roses T-shirts, paired with loose jeans. Little wonder then that I was the 'odd man out' in my company.

Om Group was my fourth employer in the last two years. My previous three employers were advertising agencies. I was recruited by Om Group's creative family and Abhi was selected by the Human Resource Family. In Om Group, departments were called 'Families' because the HR guys thought it created a sense of belonging.

————

"Hey, I thought we were the only ones travelling there," I said as we boarded the bus. I was expecting a special ride in the company vehicle, but was surprised to see more than 50 people in the bus. Most of them were new recruits. "Wasn't it supposed to be a special mission or something? Meant for just two people?" I asked Abhi.

"A special mission for just two people! I don't think so. I have heard it's some kind of mass training session, which happens regularly for new recruits. Many people will be there. I will consider myself lucky if I even get a chance to shake hands with Harry."

I was disappointed. "I thought we would be meeting Harry in person and learning from him."

"Dude, just imagine the chances of that! He is a multi-billionaire entrepreneur. Runs a conglomerate of companies. Has a presence in 14 countries. You think he will walk over to us and tell us, "Boys, will you please join me for coffee. I want to share the business strategy of Dhirubhai Ambani with you. Get real, Dave!"

"All right. All right. You are right, Mr. MBA. Now can we

please stop discussing work and get something to eat. It's an overnight journey and I am hungry."

"I have some homemade sandwiches," Abhi offered.

"No, thanks. I got some burgers from McDonalds. Also a packet of Rocher."

"Rocher? Ferrero Rocher chocolates?" Abhi's face lit up.

"Yes, there is a big packet in my bag. Have as many as you like. Got it for free!" I chuckled.

"Ferrero Rocher chocolates for free! Who gave them to you?"

"Skymark Advertising, the ad agency where I used to work before joining Om Group."

"Wow. What a wonderful company. Giving one of the world's best chocolates to employees for free!"

"No. The company did not give it to me. I got it without them realising!"

"How?" Abhi asked.

"Listen mate. Your B-school does not teach you all this. To learn such tricks you need to have a creative brain, like I do."

"Come to the point!" Abhi was annoyed now. He certainly did not approve of someone criticising his alma mater.

"Well," I started, "my ad agency used to give us a medical allowance. They would reimburse our medical expenses every month. So, I used to purchase chocolates and other such things from a medical store and include them in the invoice under the category 'General Items'. When the invoice was approved, I would get my money back."

"But that's cheating."

"It's not. The company used to make us toil our sweat and blood. What we took in return was nothing. And it wasn't me, many others used to do it too."

"And you never felt guilty about it?"

"Why should I? We never really cheated the company. We just hedged on their policies… Around two months ago, my cousin was hospitalised. His family is not financially secure. I asked him to use my name on the medical bills. My employer had to approve the expenses. He was spared the trouble of borrowing money. And I felt proud of myself because I had helped a poor fellow."

"I really don't know whether I approve of this," Abhi said, "was this a common phenomena in your company?"

"Of course, dude! It happens everywhere. In every company in the world, employees figure out innumerable ways of getting their employers to pay for every single thing. You are new. You don't have any work experience, else you would have known about these tactics."

"What else did you do?"

"Well, many of us in the office cheated on the conveyance allowance. We would travel by bus, but claim the taxi fare in our vouchers."

"And how did that help?"

"The taxi fare is much higher than the bus fare. So, we got more from the company than our expense. The difference would be our profit."

"Gosh! That is disgusting! How can you be so cheap?"

"It's not 'cheap'! It's creative! It takes some creativity to think of such ideas. And mind you, there are tonnes of such strategies I can teach you. Just be receptive."

"To hell with you and your lessons," Abhi said in disgust, pulling a blanket over himself. "I have more important assignments than looting my company. And for heaven's sake, it's an overnight journey. I suggest you get some sleep before we reach the training centre."

Abhi switched off the lights above our seats and pushed the seat back to sleep.

I was feeling a little sleepy, but I was never comfortable sleeping in a moving vehicle.

The bus was speeding along the national highway. The signboards, written in the local language made no sense to me. The only thing I could make out was that we were far from any urban settlement.

Abhi was snoring. The others too had long since dozed off. The only other person awake in the bus was the driver. I walked over to him.

"Do you want anything, sahib?"

"No thanks," I replied, relieved that we both knew enough Hindi to keep the conversation going.

"Where exactly are we going?" I asked.

"To a place called Saroon," he replied.

"Saroon," I whispered to myself. The name sounded quite familiar. I tried to recollect where I had heard it before.

"Got it!" I exclaimed. "Was this the same place devastated by an earthquake two years ago?"

"Yes, yes." He said. "Saroon was the epicenter."

Two years ago, a devastating earthquake had occurred western India, killing more than a hundred thousand people. Property and infrastructure worth crores were destroyed in seconds. Thousands of families lost everything they had. Although two years had gone by, people were still struggling to get their life back to normal.

A chill ran down my spine as I recollected pictures of the disaster. Every day the newspapers carried photos of the dead, families crying out for support, helpless children, heaps of rubble where houses used to be, and other such images that you would wish never to see in your worst nightmare.

"Saroon is where the training centre is located," the driver said. "You will be staying there."

"What?" I was shocked, finding it hard to believe that we would be training in the midst of all those ruins !

But the driver was too busy manoeuvring the bus to notice the fear in my eyes.

3

THE CHOSEN ONES

En route Saroon, we passed many towns and villages that had been destroyed by the earthquake. The partially built houses and temporarily erected structures suggested that normalcy. was yet to be restored and the locals were gradually trying to rehabilitate themselves.

But, after a few miles, I was surprised to see areas that had been completely transformed — rows of well-constructed houses on both sides of the road that had already been painted and not a single reminder of the tragedy the place had witnessed. Even the roads seemed wider and cleaner than in the rest of Saroon.

It's surprising, I thought. This place seemed to have healed itself.

"How far are we from the center?" I asked the driver.

"We are almost there. It's hardly a mile from here."

"All right then, I'd better get my bags packed. Thank you for the journey."

"You're welcome, sahib."

When I got to my seat, Abhi had just woken up.

"Did you find out where we are going, Dave?" he asked.

"To Saroon, the place that was the epicenter of the recent earthquake."

"What? Are you kidding?" Abhi asked.

"No, seriously. These guys have built a center at the heart of Saroon."

"I am not surprised," Abhi said, rubbing his eyes and straining to keep himself awake. "Property prices must have fallen after the quake, these people must've got the place cheap."

"Misers," I replied. "Always willing to cut costs wherever possible. Be it acquiring property or paying salaries. Making us work for peanuts, literally!"

The bus took a sharp turn and finally came to a stop. A few other buses were already parked in the wide open space. The driver turned off the engine and got off the bus. Before any of us could alight, a young girl hurried into the bus. She stood in front of us and announced, "Hi! My name is Saloni," she said in a bright and cheerful

voice, while she tucked a stray lock of hair behind her ear.
"On behalf of the Hospitality Family, I welcome you all. It
is a pleasure to have you here with us. Your lodging and all
other requirements have been arranged. We have a full-
fledged training hall, well-furnished rooms, a multi-cuisine
restaurant, a gymnasium, sports room, swimming pool,
and a discotheque in this facility."

"Wow!" everyone exclaimed, certainly excited to hear the
word 'discotheque' in such a remote place. The training
session and the venue sounded much better than what we
had imagined.

Saloni continued, "Yes, we have all the facilities to pamper
you. Just make yourself comfortable. We are family and
this is *your home*," she said. "Harry will address you at 9 am
in the assembly hall. And he is a strict disciplinarian, so
please ensure you are on time."

It was already 7 o'clock. I wanted to sleep before the
session, but that no longer seemed possible.

"By the way," Saloni added, "May I ask Abhi and Dave to
come with me please?"

Although I was surprised to hear her call out our names,
Abhi and I immediately waved to her, gathered our bags,
and followed her. It always felt nice to be personally
addressed by a beautiful girl.

"Well, Harry wants to meets you right away. It's urgent.

Please accompany me to his cabin," she requested. "The others can move to their rooms."

Everyone stared at us as we walked away. They were all wondering why such a high-profile businessman would seek a rendezvous with two youngsters.

"What is it about?" Abhi asked Saloni as we got off the bus. "Why does he want to meet us?"

"Yes, please tell us," I urged. "I am a little nervous."

"Well, I don't know exactly why," Saloni said slowly. "The only thing I know is that it has got something to do with the diary."

"Diary? What diary?" Abhi asked immediately.

Saloni stopped walking and looked at us carefully. "You don't know anything about the secret diary?" she asked.

"No, we don't," I replied dryly. "Now please stop this mystery business and tell us what it is."

"That diary," she said, "I have not read it, because I am not supposed to. Harry keeps it in his personal locker." And then she looked around her to see if anyone was within hearing distance. She whispered softly, "The stuff mentioned in it is priceless. You will come to know soon."

4

THE SECRET DIARY

Harry's office was in a huge white edifice. Inside, a long corridor was lined with portraits of leading entrepreneurs. The scions from the families of the Tatas, Birlas, Godrej, even Bill Gates, Warren Buffet, Rockefeller, Andrew Carnegie, and several others. Saloni led the way to Harry's office. Abhi and I had no idea what we were going to say, or what we were expected to do. Hitler had mentioned that our visit was special, but 'special' could be interpreted in many ways.

I decided to let things flow. It was just a matter of a few minutes anyway, before everything would be clear.

"Normally, we do not report to office so early," Saloni was saying. "Our day begins at 9 am. But yesterday, he specifically asked me to escort both of you to his office, before the session begins. Maybe he has something important to tell you."

We stood outside the chamber. It was a huge hall,

tastefully decorated. The entrance to his room was similar to the cabins in our Mumbai office — the glass was transparent and the door was open.

"Opaque and closed cabins detach the occupier from the staff," Sameer had said during our orientation. "Often he develops an unnecessary ego and sense of importance by making people wait for long hours to meet him. Therefore, at Om Group we follow a 'transparent policy'. There is nothing to hide from you. The organisation thrives on our mutual interaction and whenever needed, the concerned authorities are approachable," he had assured us.

I vividly remembered his words, "A psychological gap leads to misunderstandings and prejudices. Our attempt is to minimise the ego-barriers in the organisation."

Saloni knocked on the glass and sought permission to enter, we stood behind her. I was gripped by an irrational fear as soon as I saw Harry. I was still finding it hard to believe that I was meeting this legendary businessman *in person*. Harry was working on his laptop.

"He looks so different from the photos in newspapers," Abhi said softly. "He is much shorter than I thought."

He was a small man. About 5'2" tall, and in his early sixties. A pair of brown-frame glasses covered his sharp, piercing eyes. Like a typical Indian businessman, he was dressed in a safari suit.

"Come in," Harry smiled.

Abhi and I quietly walked across the length of the chamber to his desk.

"*Welcome, Welcome,*" he greeted us, getting up from his table and walking towards us. There was a sudden rush of energy and enthusiasm in his walk. We were totally taken aback by this informal behaviour.

"How are you?" he asked while pumping our hands in a firm handshake.

"We are fine, Sir," I replied, relieved at his warm welcome.

"Tch...Tch. Don't call me 'Sir'," he said in disgust. "You can call me Harry," he said placing his hand on our shoulders and squeezing it affectionately. "You see, people in western countries cannot pronounce my name, Haribhai, so they have christened me Harry."

"Sure," I blurted. I was taken aback at the way he had greeted us, as though we were his childhood friends. It really felt nice.

Saloni realised how confused we were. She knew that we were unaware of Harry's marvellous ability to instantly connect with strangers. He used, what I later realised was the power of the 'affectionate touch'. It really helped create an instant rapport with people.

"He is Abhi, and this is Dave," she said, introducing us to

Harry, like a well-mannered PA. After that she took Harry's consent to leave.

"Boys, a very warm welcome to our training centre," Harry said while indicating chairs close to his desk.

We sat down. All our apprehensions about training in a devastated earthquake-hit area, the letter from our boss hinting at the power of Bania Buddhi, and the surprise meeting with one of the greatest entrepreneurs of our time, had all faded away.

Abhi also looked pretty relaxed and comfortable. He tended to be overcautious and took his own time before opening up to any stranger. But, even he seemed to be totally mesmerised by Harry.

"Well," Harry said while adjusting his glasses, "Before I tell you what I called you here for, I want you to tell me something about yourselves."

Abhi started introducing himself, "I am Abhi Thakur, I have earned my B.Tech from IIT Delhi and an MBA from IIM Ahmedabad."

"And I am Dave Fernandes, I have earned my Bachelor of Mass Communication from St. Xavier's College. I was formerly employed with Skymark Advertising as a copywriter and was awarded the 'Best Rookie of the Year'."

"Wow! This is interesting. I had asked Deepak to give me

one MBA student and someone with excellent writing skills. Looks like he has made the perfect choice. But I want to know, did he tell you anything about the nature of your assignment?"

"No. He didn't. The only thing he told us was that we would be posted at a village in central Gujarat for the next few days," Abhi said.

"And he didn't even tell us where we were going," I added. "It was only this morning that we found out that we would be posted at Saroon."

Harry laughed. Perhaps he found my description of events amusing. "We never mention this place to anyone, till they come here for training since people have all kinds of negative ideas about this place because of the earthquake. But there is a reason why I have built a training centre here. Look at that photo."

He pointed at one of the many photographs on the wall. "You see that boy out there in the fields, the second picture from the left. That fellow is me and the place is right here in Saroon."

"I was born here," he said with pride.

"The earthquake destroyed everything in this area and in the adjoining districts," Harry continued. "The devastation was unimaginable. The locals lost everything they had. We lost some of our closest friends and our ancestral property.

I immediately sanctioned a few million rupees from our foundation, for the rehabilitation of the entire area that had been affected. But six months later, when I came here, I realised that most of the funds and aid from different trusts and foundations had been eaten up by intermediaries. Very little actually reached the needy."

"That is so disgusting," Abhi said angrily.

"Yes, it really is." Harry continued. "The locals are a deserving lot. They just needed the right catalyst. I was so touched by their plight that I decided it was time to take time off from work. I asked my son, Sameer, to take charge of Om Group and allow me to retire. Even he knew that it would be impossible to make me change my decision. So, I gave up all my formal responsibilities in Om Group and am engaged in the transformation of Saroon. We achieved remarkable results in just six months. And today, with the help of the locals we have built one of the finest townships in the country."

I remembered the horrifying images that I had seen in newspapers and the ruins on our way to Saroon. While places far away from the epicentre were still taking time to limp back to normal, the areas closer to Saroon stood out prominently. Clean roads, well-constructed and painted houses, and not a scar of destruction visible anywhere.

"Yes," I said. "I was surprised to see the development in this area while we were coming here."

"Your training centre is magnificent," Abhi added. "It is nothing short of a five-star resort."

"It is the best in the country," Harry said softly, trying to sound modest. "And it had to be. After all it was built to fulfil Dhirubhai Ambani's last dream."

"Had you met Dhirubhai Ambani?" I blurted.

"He was my first boss, and later my mentor," Harry said. "Before I floated Om Group, I was an employee in Reliance for a few years. I have seen Dhirubhai rise from a small rented office in South Mumbai and become India's richest man."

"That means you had the opportunity to see the genius at work," Abhi eyes shone brightly.

"Yes!" Harry smiled. "Few people in the world have had the privilege of learning directly from him. I was one of them! In his early years, he used to spend considerable time coaching his team. He knew he needed an army of efficient people to help him pursue his gigantic vision for Reliance. Ambani personally groomed me and transformed me from a simple clerk in his Mumbai office to the manager in his first factory in Naroda. And later on, when I decided to start my own company, he gave me a lot of support. Much of the credit of Om Group's phenomenal growth is due to the fact that we have followed the Ambani school of thought in our daily management practices."

"You told us you have built this centre to fulfil Ambani's last dream. May I know what it was?" I asked.

Harry pushed aside the papers on his table and lifted up a small box. It had a small red diary and a printed sheet in it. He quickly put the red diary inside his drawer, perhaps because he did not want us to read it, but pushed the sheet across the table, towards me.

"Here have a look at it. This is the e-mail that I sent to Deepak on the basis of which you were selected for this project."

Dear Deepak,

In 1998, when Wharton Business School awarded its prestigious Dean's Medal to Dhirubhai Ambani, he had mentioned in his speech that if this country had a thousand Dhirubhais then we would be on top of the world. Later, when I pondered over his words I realised that we have not yet taken any major steps to inculcate a spirit of entrepreneurship amongst our current generation. The new breed of youngsters in our society is immensely talented. Unlike their forefathers they do not believe earning money is a sin. Capitalism is not criticised and 'Big' is considered 'Better'. Given the appropriate environment for growth and freedom to conduct their activities, these youngsters will produce miracles.

Our Saroon Experiment has been a huge success. We have once again proved that people who work with an 'entrepreneurial mentality' achieve the best results. Other districts in the earthquake affected area that relied only on the government and bureaucratic machinery have all faced disappointment. But at Saroon, we have taught people how to take charge and work with a spirit of commitment. That is precisely the reason why they have succeeded in creating a world-class township here. But, we cannot afford to stop now. We need to reach out to the masses. I have learnt some wonderful lessons from Dhirubhai and other great entrepreneurs that I want to spread to the whole world.

You know that I have been coaching people about 'Bania Buddhi' for the last few months, but my health has been getting worse. The doctor has advised me to cease conducting workshops. This is the last batch I will be addressing. But this time the content will be different. Apart from talking to them about Bania Buddhi, I will also share with them the 'Three Secret Laws of Money' which I have never discussed before. I urgently need two young executives who can carry this legacy forward. Sameer will tell you more about it. Let me know when you choose suitable candidates.

With Love,
Haribhai 'Harry' Shah

I passed the letter to Abhi. Many things had now become clear. Harry, was a former Reliance employee and Dhirubhai had taught him how to become an entrepreneur. He had then established Om Group and by following

Ambani's lessons, Harry had achieved phenomenal success. After the earthquake had destroyed his hometown, he quit work and engaged himself in rebuilding the area. And now, he was following Ambani's dream and infusing a spirit of entrepreneurship amongst people.

"What is this 'Bania Buddhi' mentioned in the last paragraph?" Abhi asked, pointing the words out to Harry.

"Oh! Bania Buddhi! It simply means the 'wisdom of the Banias'. The Banias are one of India's most powerful business communities. Despite the fact that the original Bania traders were not highly educated, they had keen finance and business instincts. Unlike B-school students who learn in classrooms, the Banias pick up their lessons from the street. They are clever in business and have a huge appetite for risks. Most of them have created fortunes out of nothing."

"Was Dhirubhai a Bania?" I asked.

"Yes. He came from a Modh Bania family. He was only a matriculate but his understanding of markets could embarrass the best management students. When he arrived in Mumbai, he was ridiculed and called several names. Not only that, people resented an 'outsider' making money and therefore placed several obstacles in his way. Yet, Dhirubhai used clever tactics and strategies to beat away all opposition and achieve success. In fact, some of the financial and accounting decisions that he took have been unparalleled in Indian corporate history. He always insisted on using raw Bania lessons along with modern management practices in our daily work.

"And what are the 'Three Secret Laws of Money' that you have mentioned?"

Harry smiled. He looked at us and didn't speak for a while. "'The Three Secret Laws of Money' are a tool to create infinite wealth, and that too without putting in any efforts!" he finally said.

Abhi and I looked at each other. I could tell he was as curious as I was. Creating infinite wealth without putting in efforts, it sounded too good to be true.

"But let that remain a secret yet," Harry said, "I will tell you about it during the course. Right now, I want you to listen carefully to what I am going to tell you."

He pulled his chair forward, took off his glasses, and spoke to us in a stern voice, "Boys, this is serious business and I want religious obedience from you. I have been spreading Dhirubhai's wisdom like an evangelist for the last four years. But, the world is too big for me to address alone. And, I don't have many years left. My health is getting worse. Hence, I have decided that it's time to select worthy successors who can take this forward. I wanted one person who has excellent writing skills and one person who can design a B-school type course module. Keeping this in mind, I asked Deepak to give me a good writer and a B-school student. And that is why the two of you have been selected."

He paused, while we drew in our breath.

"We will capitalise on your core competencies. Since Dave has been a copywriter, his job will be to condense the entire training session into a written manuscript which we will publish later. This published material will be circulated to millions of people. And since Abhi has been a trainer, his job will be to design a course module and spread the philosophy to B-schools, management students, and corporate houses. My race is now over and I am passing the baton to you. The legacy is all yours. Is that clear?"

"Well, er..." I stuttered. "Are you sure we are the perfect people? I mean we are still junior level employees. Amateurs. And such a huge responsibility on our shoulders...?"

Harry interrupted, "I insisted on amateurs. A professional would have seen this project as a part of his routine. It would be something very much within his domain. But, *you* will have to stretch to grasp it. And that is what I want. *If you ask a person to do something within his grasp, he will see it as work, but if he is inspired to do something beyond his grasp, he will pursue it as a challenging quest.*"

Abhi smiled. His eyes gleamed with admiration for Harry's wisdom. "I assure you sir, we will do it," he said confidently. "We are proud of your faith in us and we will not disappoint you."

"Oh wonderful! That's like my boys!" he laughed with pride. "I knew you would agree."

I tried to smile, still unsure about everything.

"So let us not waste time, we will get working on this right away," Harry said. "I will see you at 9 am, in the training hall. You still have an hour to get yourselves ready. And remember to keep this conversation confidential."

"Yes, we will," I assured him.

We rose from our chairs and shook hands with Harry. Harry smiled at us affectionately. He appeared very relieved.

We walked out of his chamber, our hearts beating really quickly.

THE SHIFT

By a quarter to nine, all the participants were seated in the training hall. The Om Group employees were yawning and drowsy, thanks to the overnight bus journey. But there were several others who had arrived earlier and looked wide-eyed and alert.

Abhi and I occupied seats in the first row, intending to grab the most value from the seminar. We had decided that Abhi would try to summarise Harry's words in PowerPoint presentations, while I would take down his words for the manuscript. Saloni began the seminar with an introduction of Haribhai. A short film on his life was shown. Like us, many others were surprised when they found out Harry's association with Reliance, and his connection with Saroon.

At exactly 9 am, Harry walked through the main entrance. A cordless microphone was neatly clipped to his collar and the small red diary was in his right hand. I was eager to know what it contained. Curious eyes followed him as he walked to the platform.

"A very good morning to all of you," he began. "On behalf of Om Group, I, Haribhai Shah, or Harry as I would like you to call me, welcome you all. It is a privilege to have you here. Apart from members of Om Group, we also have among us many executives from other companies."

I took out my shorthand pen and started jotting down his words. From here onwards follows the summary of his speech as I transcribed it.

"I welcome you all to this training session. As you must have seen in the video, I have worked directly under Dhirubhai Ambani. This training programme incorporates much of the wisdom I acquired from him in my early years. But, no amount of training will have an impact on you, unless you are receptive. And receptivity can be ensured only if you get the shift. Let me begin with a story.

"Once upon a time two friends decided to join the army. They were recruited at a monthly salary of about Rs 10,000. Both of them were equally brave and skilled at handling weapons. Their careers progressed on parallel tracks, until one day, one of them decided to quit and start his own security agency. He was confident of his entrepreneurial abilities and wanted to express it fully. Time went by and he kept on expanding his activities. His dedication and commitment bore fruit. And within a few years, he achieved a market capitalisation of Rs 100 crore.

"Meanwhile, his other friend, who was still in the army, was tired of the monotonous routine and voluntarily resigned. He started working in a private firm. Both of them had lost touch with each other, until they met many years later. They were overjoyed to see each other after a long time. The whole evening was spent reliving memories of the days they had spent together. Nostalgic reminiscences flowed over glasses of wine.

" 'But I don't understand one thing,' the retired army officer asked. "We both started our careers together, both of us earned the same salary, both of us were equally talented. Yet, today you own a company worth crores and I am still an employee struggling with my finances. What exactly changed our destinies?' "

The businessman placed a consoling hand on his friend's shoulder and replied, 'Don't be offended my friend, but I would like to remind you of an incident during our early training period. After a hectic day at work, we were walking back to our dorm. I suddenly remembered that we had forgotten to switch off the fans in the office. I suggested that we go back and switch it off. But, you said there was no need to do that. It was the government's loss, you said. I insisted, but you were adamant. Ultimately, I walked back half a mile to the office and you went straight to the dorm to sleep. Well, that day, when I turned back and you walked on, it was decided who would be an entrepreneur and who would be an employee. From the very beginning, I had, what is called, the 'ownership mentality'. For me wasting the army's resources, was my own loss. I considered the army as my own institution. And from the very beginning you were operating from an 'alien mentality'. For you, it was the government's loss. Although our salaries were the same, my thoughts matched those of the 'entrepreneur-type' while yours was that of the 'employee-type'. Our different destinies as they are today are the natural consequence of our different mentalities that we exhibited years ago.'"

Harry paused. He drank some water. The silence in the auditorium was absolute. People were thinking about what they had just heard. "There are two types of people in the world," he continued, "those who are 'employee-types' and those who are 'entrepreneur-types'. Please note that I am not using the words 'entrepreneurs' and 'employees.' Instead, I am using the words 'entrepreneur-types' and 'employee types'. There is a distinction here. *There are people who are entrepreneurs, yet they have an 'employee-type' mentality and there are employees and yet they have an 'entrepreneur-type' mentality.* Whether you are an employee or an entrepreneur, makes no difference. What counts is what mentality you have — that of an entrepreneur, or one of an employee.

"In the story that I just told you, even when the businessman was employed in the army, his mind was typical of the entrepreneur-type. He couldn't tolerate a fan being operated unnecessarily and would pull his entire being into action till he switched it off. While the other friend lazily walked over the idea, leaving it to the government. Remember, *an efficient civilisation is the one which creates, nurtures, and leverages on its entrepreneur-types.*

He used a cordless remote to start a slideshow on the screen behind him. The slide read: THE SHIFT

Now, people had started whispering to each other. Almost all the participants had heard this term several times in Om Group, but didn't know what it meant.

"When we talk about 'The Shift'," Harry continued, "we mean a change in one's paradigm from employee-type to entrepreneur-type. It includes a person's attitude, mentality and behaviour.

"When I came to Saroon after the earthquake, I was really unhappy to see the place in ruins. But what really disturbed me was that the people were all behaving like 'employee-types'. Many days had gone by since the disaster had struck and they were still cursing God, cursing nature, and cursing the government. They were desperately waiting for some messiah to help them. None of them wanted to bring about change by themselves. Typical employee-type behaviour. I could understand their sentiments, but the general mentality had been corrupted. If a person found somebody who had to bear more losses than him, he would feel happy! We gave a huge sum as charity, but there was hardly any change. When I visited Saroon, with my team, I realised what the problem was. An entrepreneur-type was missing. Therefore, we decided to handle the whole situation like a businessman would. The first couple of days were spent training people. We had to make them shift their attitude, from that of an employee-type to that of an entrepreneur-type. We provided the resources, but re-building was their responsibility. We set targets, decided on deadlines, and made the locals answerable for their goals. Initially, they did not like our way at all. Working under deadlines was a headache and being answerable to someone affected their ego. They were unwilling to make any effort and wanted some NGO or trust to do the whole thing for them. But we were adamant. We would provide resources only if they worked for themselves.

"Gradually the shift took place. Their attitude started changing. They realised that they were the best people to re-build their own town. My team was just acting as a catalyst. Slowly, they took over the whole thing. *Adversity always gives birth to natural leaders.* Many young people came forward. A vision was planned, hierarchies were formed, and most importantly, rewards were given only against performance. We were deaf to criticism and continued working according to our own style. And believe it or not, in the shortest time possible we created one of the world's best townships from scratch. Today, Saroon stands as an envious example for the districts around it."

A huge round of applause greeted Harry's words.

"And I don't take credit for it," he continued, "it is the people who have done it themselves. My only job was to create the shift. Once that took place, once the entrepreneur-types were created, the system started working on its own. And in this process not only did we create an excellent township, but also a force of self-confident and able individuals. We created a class of people who now have a vision with which to lead their lives, a passion for development and a strong insistence on self-support. Rest assured, if another earthquake strikes, they will re-create the whole thing on their own. *This is the mark of a true entrepreneur, he first sets up a system and then empowers it to work independent of him."*

Another round of applause followed. The slide behind him changed and we were shown pictures of the town before and after the earthquake. The transformation was indeed unbelievable.

"When we were still a small team in Reliance, Dhirubhai once explained what his Orbit Theory was all about. According to him, in life, we move ahead in orbits. When Ambani was a petrol pump attendant he occupied one orbit. At that level he had a specific set of problems and opportunities. When he broke free from that orbit and became a clerk, he moved to a higher orbit. At that level he attracted a different set of problems and opportunities. When he broke free from that orbit and became a trader, once again the problems, opportunities, people, and circumstances were different. As he advanced to higher orbits, the elements in those orbits started revolving around him.

"When a person has an employee-type attitude, he is constantly choosing to remain in the lower orbits. In the lower orbits he will always be surrounded by scarcity in every form. Life will be very ordinary. Only when he shifts his attitude to that of an entrepreneur can he prepare to advance to higher orbits and experience true prosperity in every form. Life will be extraordinary. Whether he moves or not, depends on his actions, but first, the attitude has to change, only then can one take the appropriate actions.

"I will illustrate this point. Let's look at the differences between 'employee-types' and 'entrepreneur-types'. The very basic difference is related to change. When an employee-type has to change, he will try to avoid it as much as possible, but when an entrepreneur-type has to change, he will do so willingly. In fact, he will be the initiator of change.

"Although this logic sounds very obvious, it is not so common in practice. For years, the government-owned companies avoided computers because their staff did not know how to operate them. They preferred working on paper. In a few years, the amount of work had increased to such an extent that computers became inevitable. The government spent a lot of money on training. But, the staff was just not willing to learn. In some departments, the staff went on strike and protested against the use of computers. Some people destroyed computers because they were 'aliens' who would eat up their jobs. Can you imagine the level of resistance? Going on strike against upgradation?

"I often give the 'Bill Gates example' to our employees who are afraid of learning technology. Bill Gates was in school when he first saw a computer. In those days it was an expensive machine. A typical older family member would have thought about the huge financial investment a computer required and would keep boys away from meddling with it. But, perhaps his family was not like that. They were perhaps entrepreneur-types and encouraged him to explore the new machine fearlessly.

"If Bill Gates had crashed his first PC," Harry said emphatically, "his loss would have been a thousand-odd dollars. But, had the fear of crashing prevented him from experimenting, he would have never earned $50 billion! *The cost of not changing, is always higher than the price of change.*"

"Wow! That is some example," Abhi whispered, as I wrote it down. Abhi wanted to collect such quotes for his training module.

"Because of his eagerness to change, an entrepreneur-type is constantly awake, alert, and dynamic. He is constantly on the lookout for opportunities of growth. He cannot afford to stop at any moment. On the other hand, an employee-type becomes complacent after he achieves a certain level of growth. He then refuses to move forward.

"Some time back, Ratan Tata acquired the steel firm Corus. It is the largest acquisition by any Indian till date. He is already 70 years old, has no children, and yet at this ripe age he incessantly continues to take his company forward. How many people, at the age of 70, will have that kind of energy and the willingness to get up from their chair, forget planning the acquisition of a company. And Tata did not stop there. He went on to acquire Jaguar and Land Rover within a few months. And then he created Nano, the world's cheapest car. Despite such landmark achievements, Tata still believes a lot can be done and that a hundred years from now, Tata will be much bigger.

"The way I see it, *an entrepreneur-type never grows old, and an employee-type is hardly ever young.*"

A new slide appeared on the screen now, and it showed the current year's calendar.

"Look at the calendar. When an employee-type looks at the calendar, he will look for the dates that are red. It happens subconsciously. He is looking for holidays so that he can laze around. But, when an entrepreneur-type looks at a calendar, he will look for the dates that are black. He is looking for days of productivity that will help him increase sales, profits, and growth. Observe how at a simple act, such as looking at the calendar, both type exhibit such different behaviour. It is such a small act, yet it means so much. Though everybody wants wealth, an employee-type wants wealth without putting in any effort, but an entrepreneur-type knows wealth flows only as a consequence of efforts.

"It is not tough to find out who belongs to which type. One might try to hide his or her real feelings, but the words they use, will tell you the truth. Take a look at this chart, it compares the words chosen by both groups to express how they see their tasks and goals."

EMPLOYEE-TYPE	ENTREPRENEUR-TYPE
Bunking office	Creating wealth
Strikes	Adding value
Exploiting juniors	Encouraging ideas
False vouchers	Adapting to change
Office politics	Incessant growth
Passing the buck	Instilling professionalism
Avoiding responsibility	Increasing profitability

"When you listen to those with an employee-type attitude, they often use phrases such as 'bunking office', 'going on strike', 'exploiting juniors', 'making false vouchers', 'playing politics in office', 'passing the buck', 'avoiding responsibility', 'eagerly waiting for lunch break', etc. Through the day, their mind will be occupied with selfish, short-term thoughts. Such people are in a lower orbit, so only ideas related to that orbit will occur to them. However, once they shift their attitude to that of the entrepreneur-type, subconsciously the vocabulary changes and phrases such as 'creating wealth', 'adding value', 'encouraging ideas', 'adapting to change', 'incessant growth', 'instilling professionalism', 'increasing sales and profitability', 'pouncing on opportunities', etc, get added. All the time, the mind will be filled with thoughts of innovation and excellence."

"But, how can he expect a mere labourer to think in terms of professionalism and excellence?" Abhi asked me.

"Shh. Let him finish talking. We will ask him later," I whispered.

"I will give you a copy of this chart before the session ends. I want you to ponder over it before you come back tomorrow. Here is another one. Take a look at this chart as well. It pretty much sums up what I am trying to put across."

EMPLOYEE-TYPE	ENTREPRENEUR-TYPE
Resists change	Accepts change and often initiates it
Works for mere survival	Works for growth
Afraid of risks	Undertakes risky projects with strong belief in self
Remains in solitude	Loves to expand own network
Wants everything free of cost	Knows everything worth possessing commands a price
Is concerned only with his/her own job and salary	Has an overall view of things

EMPLOYEE-TYPE	ENTREPRENEUR-TYPE
Believes in putting in minimal efforts for salary	Believes in giving more than what they are paid
Is concerned only with the immediate	Has a long-term vision
Is jealous when others earn more money and curses them	Is jealous of other people earning money and strives to advance by elevating his/her own level of competence
Hates advice, keeps on repeating mistakes, is unwilling to learn, discourages feedback	Seeks advice, learns from mistakes, ever-willing to learn, and encourages feedback

"I will give you a minute to go through this chart and then if you have any questions, let me hear them. Do not hesitate. I am your coach and duty-bound to address your concerns.

"Harry, I have a question," Abhi stood up. "How can we expect a mere labourer to think in terms of professionalism and excellence? All this is senior-executive level stuff. It is meant for executives, not for him."

"No!" Harry screamed, loud enough to deafen us.

"*It is not because he is a mere labourer that he is not*

expected to think in terms of professionalism and excellence. It is because he is not thinking in terms of professionalism and excellence that he is a mere labourer. And, it is not because they are senior level executives that they are expected to think in terms of professionalism and excellence. It is because they are thinking in terms of professionalism and excellence that they are senior-level executives!

"Who decides whether a person will end up becoming a labourer in a factory, or the owner of a multinational? Is it decided at birth? No, as life takes shape, we all acquire a certain attitude and perspective towards things. This determines the direction our life will take."

He opened a page from the red diary.

"How many of you know the story of how Ambani made his first bucks?

No one raised their hand.

"I will tell you. Dhirubhai Ambani began his career as a petrol pump attendant in Yemen. Like any other attendant, his job was restricted to filling petrol in cars, and running small errands for his boss. A typical blue-collar job. Yet, his creative brain was always looking out for opportunities. Anything related to wealth and the economy would interest him. One day, he discovered that the content of silver in the currency, the Rial, was higher than the actual value of the coin. That gave him an idea. He started collecting these silver coins and melted them to make silver ingots.

He would sell these ingots to the bullion dealers in the London market. This would lead to pure profits! Initially, the margin was low, but Ambani enjoyed the arbitrage game. As time went by, he started ordering more and more of these coins. It so happened that eventually the coins started disappearing from the market. Traders were facing a shortage of Rials in their daily transactions. The complaints reached the government. Even they were stunned. They found out that a young Indian had placed an unlimited order on Rials. He was melting the coins and making money. Ultimately, they were forced to change the silver content in the coin. A young Indian shook the entire government of a foreign country!"

Harry looked at Abhi and spoke softly.

"Everything in life is a matter of choice. It doesn't mean that you must think in a particular way if you are at a certain level. Ambani, too, was a mere labourer. There were thousands of others like him. Yet, he consciously chose to look for opportunities for creating wealth and he succeeded.

"But what about destiny?" an elderly gentleman argued. "Ambani was lucky, but everybody cannot be successful. Some people are destined to remain below average all their lives."

"Ha! Destiny may have some role to play in our lives, but it is the favourite excuse of failures. They use it to hide their inability to accomplish anything. People are strange, if they get success, the credit goes to them. But if they fail, destiny is responsible!"

He walked over to the whiteboard and wrote something with a marker pen.

CREATION BELIEVES IN CONTINUOUS EVOLUTION...

"Who said this?"

"Darwin," we all said together.

"Yes, Darwin, the scientist. But there is one little known quote by a man called Antonio Gaudi. I will write it down for you."

CREATION CONTINUES INCESSANTLY THROUGH THE MEDIA OF MAN

He looked at the gentleman and asked, "I want you to look at the two quotes for a minute. Don't assume that they are two separate statements. Join them and tell me what you see."

There was silence in the auditorium. Everyone was interpreting it their own way. After a few seconds, the old man said, "Creation advances using man as a medium."

"Yes, creation uses us to advance. If the sole purpose of creation is to 'advance' and if we are its 'highest medium', why would it stop us from getting ahead?"

"I got it!" the gentleman smiled.

"Thank you," Harry said.

"I will end today's session with a very meaningful Zen story. I want you to ponder over it. *People consciously remain in lower orbits and yet blame destiny for not 'allowing' them to advance ahead.* This story is dedicated to such people..."

Everybody sat up straight. Stories were something everyone loved to listen. And Harry used them beautifully to highlight his message.

"A poor boy once approached a Zen monk and said, 'Master, my name is Lin. I want to be the richest and most successful man in China. But, I come from a poor peasant family. I have no formal education. My parents don't have enough money to provide proper food and clothing. I want to rise to great heights in life, but everyone says that my family has always been like this and I am destined to be a failure all my life. O Learned One, please tell me, will I ever succeed in transforming myself?'

"Lin waited impatiently for the master to answer, but there was no response. The master summoned three of his most trusted disciples and whispered something in their ears. The disciples went away. A few minutes later the first disciple came back. He was carrying a small pot with some water in it. The water was crystal clear.

"After some time, the second disciple came back. He too was carrying a small pot with water but, as Lin saw, it was dirty water.

"Finally the last disciple returned. In one hand he was carrying a small pot of water and with the other hand he had covered his nose. As he entered the monastery, the other disciples moved back a few steps. From the pot came the most disgusting stink of sewage water.

"Everybody was confused. They had no idea what the master was up to. But the master said nothing and indicated that Lin and the other disciples should walk out of the monastery.

"In the open ground outside the monastery, the disciples made three piles of wooden logs and set the three pots on fire. The water started boiling.

"Everybody looked on in silence, unsure of what they were witnessing. Lin did not know what to say. After a few hours, the master asked his disciples to extinguish the fire. He walked towards Lin and asked, 'What do you see in the first pot?' 'It's empty,' replied Lin. 'How did it become empty?'

"'The water transformed into vapour.'

"'Good. What about the second pot? What happened to the water in it?'

"'It too became vapour. The pot is empty.'

"'And what about the third pot, Lin?'

"'Obviously, even that water turned to vapour. What's the big deal? Any water will be transformed if you heat it.'

"'Ahh...there you are...' the master replied, 'you just answered your own question.'

"And turning towards all his disciples, he said, 'Any human being will be transformed if you heat him. All that you need is burning desire. Transformation is a process. It is not dependant on any element. Immaterial of the element, the process will always work. The first pot was filled with the purest water from the source of river Yangtse. The second pot was filled with the dirty water. And the third pot was filled with water from the sewage pipe outside the village. As long as the water was in the pot, it was bound by its destiny. The pure water would shine and the sewage water would stink. That was its destiny. But immaterial of its different form it was able to transform itself to vapour. Similarly, our different backgrounds give us different destinies. Some people are born in affluent families. Some people are born in mediocre families. Whilst, some, like Lin are born in extremely sympathetic conditions. But, *the process of transformation is not at all related to destiny. It applies uniformly to everyone.*'

"Anybody who is ready to undergo the process will be able to transform himself and rise to greater, unbounded heights, as the water in the pot.

"Remember," Harry said as the day's session came to an end, *"transformation is available to you, right now."*

———

A MAN'S DREAMS ARE AN INDEX TO HIS GREATNESS
—ZADOK RABINWITZ

That night as I thought about Harry's words, a strange emotion gripped me. Coming from a typical middle-class family, all I had known since childhood was that I was average. Everything in our life was average. Our lifestyle, our possessions, our joys, our passions, our celebrations, everything was average. And there were countless others like me who were living within our limited perceptions of mediocrity.

We were not permitted lavishness of any sort. It was considered a sin. Wealthy and successful people were supposed to be from another world. A world we could never reach.

I knew that like my elders I too had to get a 'safe and secure job' and support my family. That was the only goal in my life. To get a good job that paid well. There was no scope for pursuing my dreams, and doing what I loved to do. I was burdened under such heavy expectations that I had forgotten entirely the delights of dreaming.

On one hand was my entire past, screaming to me that I was destined to be just average. And on the other hand was Harry's voice urging me to consider that 'an opportunity of transformation was always available'.

Like the water that had turned to vapour and rose above, I, too, could reach out to the skies.

TUNING YOUR MIND

On the second day, people occupied their chairs well before time. They were eagerly waiting for the session to begin. Unlike other self-improvement seminars that were usually boring, Harry's innovative use of stories and anecdotes was very captivating. He would have the crowd glued to its seats for as long as he spoke.

"Any shift in the world," Harry began, "takes place in two stages. The first stage is distinction and the second stage is displacement. If I want to shift this chair from here to there, then first there has to be a distinction. I must distinguish two separate points. And then there must be displacement, the chair must actually be moved from one point to another.

"Now consider this chair as a symbol representing you. We have already distinguished between two separate points — the employee and entrepreneur attitude. All of you have understood this. What is needed now is displacement, which will involve actually shifting from one attitude to another. But it is not going to be easy. You will encounter a lot of resistance at first.

"People love being the 'employee-type'. They love resisting change, having fun in office, boosting their own ego, and surviving on the company's finances. There is so much fun in holding on to these peanuts that in the process they confine their whole existence.

"I will give you an example from real life. Do you know how they catch monkeys in India? The monkey-catcher uses cages that have a narrow opening. He places a peanut or a banana in the cage. When the monkey comes down, he slides his hand through the narrow door and holds the peanut in his fist. But, because of the narrow opening, he is not able to get his fist out. Now the monkey has two options — to let go of the peanut and slide his hand out, or to hold on the peanut but be trapped in the cage.

"Guess what? The desire to cling on to the peanut is so strong that the monkey risks his entire existence for that small snack. He clings on to the peanut and the hunter is easily able to catch him!

"I often give this example to make people realise how by focusing on 'petty things' we lose out on bigger things in life.

"When I was Ambani's manager, I used to make false vouchers. I would travel in the second class but, in the voucher I would say 'travelled by first class'. The difference in the fares was my profit. If I had to take a personal photocopy of documents, or many printouts I would use the company's facilities. When my daughter got married, I issued about 100 invitations through the office phone. The company was my first port of call for all these extra activities. And I loved this game very much, it was free money."

Abhi kicked me hard, perhaps to remind me of the free Ferrero Rochers and the argument we had had in the bus.

"Then, one day, I had to go to a rural area for field work. In my voucher I claimed taxi fare. Actually, I had travelled in a bus. But, it had become a habit to lie all the time. The accountant presented my voucher to Dhirubhai with a note: 'There are no taxis in the place he visited'.

"When I came to know of it, I thought Dhirubhai would definitely be angry. We were a small team then and he knew every employee personally. Dhirubhai disapproved my voucher, but did not say anything.

"For a couple of days I waited, but he did not raise the matter. On the third day, I apologised to him. The guilt was unbearable.

"'Please forgive me,' I said, 'I am sorry.'

"He put aside the files on his table and the way he looked at me suggested that he wasn't angry, but upset with me.

"He said, 'I know that some of my staff members use the company's resources for their personal benefit. If I want to I can spend my time checking every voucher and running behind people to catch them every time they cheat. But, if I spend time doing all that when will I get the time to pursue my vision for Reliance? I want to make Reliance one of the best companies in the country and that is what I am focussing on. I cannot afford to put my vision at stake in order to save a few hundred rupees every month. Do you understand?'

"'Yes,' I replied. My head still bowed down in shame.

"'All this time you have only been cheating yourself. Your mind is focused on ways by which you can extract extra benefits from the company. And you have even succeeded in doing so. But remember, the mind works like a radio. If you tune it to a lower frequency, it will attract ideas of a lower frequency. If you tune it to a higher frequency, it will attract ideas of a higher frequency. All this time, it has been tuned to a lower frequency. You were thinking of small, small ways by which you could leak into the company's cash flows. And this was so delightful that you continued doing it. But you only got benefits worth peanuts. Had you tuned your mind to a higher frequency, and stopped running after peanuts then you would have attracted an entire new realm of opportunities.'

"I nodded my head, trying to show that I understood.

"'When I was a petrol pump attendant in Yemen, there were thousands of others like me. Our job was to fill petrol in cars. My colleagues spent their whole day running after rich customers and collecting additional tips. Their mind was only tuned to the idea of collecting additional tips. Extracting more and more from rich customers was the only goal in their life. And because they succeeded, they kept repeating their behaviour. On the other hand, I spent my time observing the local markets and merchants. I was constantly studying the trade of Yemen. I consciously decided not to run after tips and instead tuned my mind to a higher frequency. And as time passed I had a precise idea of how I could profit from arbitrage between the Indian and Yemen trade markets. I knew exactly what was to be exported, what was to be imported, and what my margins would be. Today, I own an import-export business and I make excellent profits. My former colleagues are perhaps still filling petrol in cars. By consciously deciding not to run after peanuts I created new opportunities for myself. Even in the Rial, I saw what no one else did. Some people call it luck. But it is not so. *Luck arises when opportunity meets preparedness.* My mind was prepared to receive and therefore I succeeded. And because my mind is tuned to the highest frequency, it keeps giving me the best ideas. Right now, in our import-export markets, the profits are good. Traders in the market are enjoying it and holding on to the money. But, very soon we will move on to manufacturing. Because in manufacturing, the profits are much higher. I have noticed an excellent opportunity in the polyester market which people have ignored. But, we are going to move on completely.'

"I was listening to him, my head still bowed down. I did not have the courage to look at him.

"'You can continue thinking of innovative ways of using the company's resources for your personal benefit,' he continued. 'But, the cost is that you will be stuck all your life chasing peanuts. When you get promoted you will get bigger peanuts. But they are all peanuts. By holding on to them you are depriving yourself of hundreds of other opportunities that float around you every day. Since your mind is tuned to a lower frequency it will just not attract higher ideas.'

"He swivelled in his chair and thrust his body forward, 'Or you have another option. You may decide to quit such practices and align yourself to the company's vision. That would mean not engaging in 'time pass' in the office and committing yourself to continuously create wealth for the company. And once you start creating wealth for the company, you will master the art of wealth creation. You will realise that wealth has its laws. And the same laws that you use to create wealth for the organisation can be used to create wealth for yourself. In an attempt to make the company wealthier, you will learn the art of making yourself wealthier.'

"I stared at Dhirubhai. His words hit me hard. Prior to that day, I was only hacking into the company's wealth. I had never learnt how to create wealth. Perhaps that was the reason why money was an eternal problem for me. I always had to endure a financial struggle. Immaterial of how much money I hacked, yet the struggle seemed eternal.

"Dhirubhai looked into my eyes and was sure that I had got his message. He got up from his chair and placed an arm around my shoulder affectionately and went away."

Harry paused. He walked forward a couple of steps and stood right at the edge of the stage, and said, "That day changed my life. That day I decided I would stop looting the organisation and commit myself fully to its growth. I stopped making false vouchers; I stopped fooling around in office and started thinking about ways by which I could create wealth for my company. Slowly, I learnt the art of creating wealth. I learnt the laws of money and how it behaves. I learnt the secrets of success and growth, which are not mentioned anywhere else.

"The reason why I have called you here is to teach all of you how to create wealth and how to be successful. It has nothing to do with morality and ethics. It is a precise science which anybody can master. But, for that you will have to stop chasing peanuts. Peanut chasers cannot create real wealth.

"From being just a small employee in Reliance, I grew to be the owner of one of the country's top 100 companies. I want to teach you the same secrets that I learnt. During my tenure in Reliance, I used to observe Dhirubhai's style of working and note down whatever I could understand."

Harry showed us the red diary that he carried with him wherever he went. People stared at it eagerly.

"I have preserved this diary for more than four decades. The stuff mentioned in it is priceless. Apart from some general techniques on developing personal effectiveness, it contains Ambani's personal wisdom for success and wealth creation. For years I did not speak about it, because I felt the time was not right. In those days, talking about wealth was considered a sin. Earning money was bad. But now things have changed. Our society has become wealth-conscious and money is rightly respected. But to understand the contents of this diary you will have to raise your level of thinking. It will not happen at the level of 'Actions.' It will happen at the level of 'Being'. Take a look at this slide."

I took out my diary. It was time to take notes.

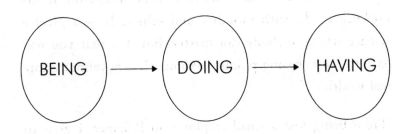

"There are three circles. In the first circle is the word 'Being'. From it, an arrow leads to 'Doing' and from there, an arrow leads to 'Having'. What are these three words — 'Being', 'Doing', and 'Having'?"

"Verbs," somebody said loudly.

"Yes, of course they are verbs. But there is a special relationship between them," Harry added. "'Being' suggests who you are. It is related to your level of personal competence and excellence. 'Doing' relates to all the actions that you take and 'Having' relates to the results you get. In other words, your being determines what you do, which in turn determines what you have. It is not the actions but the Self which is the source of all achievements. All actions flow from the Self.

"The problem with us is that whenever we want to 'Have' success or wealth we only focus on what actions we should take, without working on our Self, our 'Being'. But all 'Doing' flows from the 'Being' because it is only the Self that can take action. As long as one does not elevate their own personal competency and level of excellence, all actions are bound to be mediocre.

"Let me illustrate this point with a story which is famous with sailors. Once a vessel loaded with cargo was on a journey, but developed a mechanical fault. The crew tried their best but found the problem too complicated to solve. The Captain ordered the vessel to be anchored and the crew got together a couple of mechanics. These mechanics also did not succeed. Finally, a young lad presented himself. As soon as he entered the ship, he asked the crew to take him to the lower deck. Amidst the large maze of pipes, he selected a particular one and hit it five times with his hammer. And the problem was solved! The crew and the Captain were surprised. He made it look so easy. The Captain thanked him and said, 'We are proud of you, young man. Tell us what are your fees?'

" 'A thousand dollars,' the youth replied.

" 'A thousand dollars! That's a lot of money for a two-minute job.'

" 'Yes, it is.'

" 'How do you justify your demand?'

" 'It's simple,' replied the mechanic, 'Five cents for hitting the pipe five times and $999.95 for knowing where to hit.' "

All the participants laughed and nodded.

"Hitting a pipe five times can be done by anyone, but the knowledge of where exactly one must strike is the outcome of ability and excellence. This is precisely what gave the boy the edge over others in the same field.

"You will find such people in every strata of society. I have met lawyers who charge only Rs 1000 per consultation and yet find it difficult to get business, while lawyers who charge millions per consultation are booked for months in advance. They have studied from the same books, in the same university, under the same professor. Their 'Doing' is the same, but because their 'Being' is different, they have different outcomes.

"Don't we know of other professionals — doctors, actors, scientists, sportsmen — some of them have earned a good reputation around the world, and some of them struggle all their life to achieve even the slightest recognition. Look at any choreographed group dance in a Bollywood movie. Though all the women are dancing just like the lead actress, it is the lead who gets paid thousand times more than the other 'extras' dancing behind her. The dance, the music, the choreography, the set, everything is the same for the extras and the lead. But the lead has higher recognition and hence gets higher rewards.

"I will give you an example from Om Group. About three years ago, we were planning to acquire a loss-making unit. A consultant was needed who would turn the unit around and create profits. We got applications from many managers, but their profile was not impressive. One consultant, however, seemed to be an expert in handling such cases. But, the fees he demanded were very high. Initially, I was reluctant, but then I remembered Dhirubhai's words. He used to say, *'If you throw peanuts, you attract monkeys. If you want to attract genuine talent you have to willingly pay the price it commands'*. I hired him. And guess what? Within a few months he had the whole unit back on track. He reduced the losses, motivated the staff, introduced new technology and gave a positive momentum to the company's growth. The value addition that he contributed through his work was much more than what we paid him. He deserved the price that he commanded.

Harry removed his glasses and started wiping them clean while still talking, "I really want you to get this," he said. "If you develop your competency, money and opportunity will seek you rather than you chasing them. Even luck will be in your favour. Luck tends to be attracted towards talent. Perhaps that was the reason why Gibbon said that *'the wind and waves are always on the side of the ablest navigators'*."

"Wow! What a powerful statement!" Abhi whispered as he jotted it down.

"And that is precisely why Pareto's principle works," Harry went on, "do you know what it is?"

A few people nodded.

"Pareto's principle is also called the '80:20 principle'. The core idea is that 80 percent of the wealth in any society revolves around just 20 percent of the people, and 20 percent of society's wealth revolves around 80 percent of the people. Since a majority of people in any society live in only two dimensions — doing and having — their whole world comprises 'taking actions' and 'having results'. There is very little or no 'Being' involved. Most of their work is routine and repetitive. Once a certain pattern is set, they just repeat it through their lives without ever bothering to increase their competency. So they have to satisfy themselves with little wealth. But the other 20 percent have a third dimension to their life — 'Being'. And do you know what the third dimension gives?" he asked expectantly.

Nobody knew.

"Suppose there is a two-dimensional object and a three-dimensional object. What is the difference between the two?" Harry asked.

Still no response.

"A 2-D object has length and breadth, but a 3-D object has length, breadth and...?"

"Height!" we all said aloud.

"Yes, exactly," Harry smiled, "the third dimension gives you height. The more you work on your Being the higher you rise. Perhaps that is the reason why we are called Human 'Beings'. No other animal is called a Being. Only human beings have the privilege because other creatures cannot increase their competency like we do."

A lot of what Harry was saying was now answering my life-held questions. Back in college, a professor used to tell us, *'If you have eight hours to chop a tree, then spend six hours sharpening the saw'*. With a sharpened saw, you could easily cut through the bark. Perhaps the Being was also about sharpening oneself, albeit on an ongoing basis.

Harry told us how he worked on his personal competencies. He had read tonnes of literature on wealth creation. In his chamber were portraits of the world's greatest entrepreneurs and he visualised living in their presence. Despite a hectic schedule, he would spend some time on yoga and meditation. Not only individuals, but even organisations have to work on their competencies. Om Group maintained its competency by spending huge amounts on R&D and investing on the best people and technology.

All of what Harry said confirmed whatever little understanding I had of one's Being. But then the conversation took an altogether different route and it left me quite surprised. It all began with my colleague, Sam, asking him a question.

"Harry, you mentioned people who hack into the company's finances for their personal gains, but what about those groups of people who officially seek free reservations and quotas from the government? They don't want to work on their Being, they just want readymade solutions. What is your opinion on this?"

There was silence in the auditorium for some time. Then Harry answered, "Young man, you have asked me a very profound question. If our people implement this one maxim correctly, then you have no clue what an amazing transformation we can create in this world."

"What maxim?" Sam asked humbly.

Harry picked up a marker pen and wrote in huge letters — *'THERE ARE NO FREE LUNCHES'*.

He wrote over the same words, over and over again, making the words darker, perhaps to add emphasis.

"There is a cafe in IIM Ahmedabad called 'Cafe Tanstaafl'. The word Tanstaafl loosely means – 'There are no free lunches'. And if I were to explain its meaning like a true Bania, I would say, 'Don't give anything for free to people; they will not value it. And don't seek anything free of cost; it will affect your Being'.

"Remember Dr. Mikao Usui, who invented Reiki, the alternate healing system? When Dr. Usui first started applying the techniques of Reiki on people he produced astonishing results. His patients were cured of many diseases where traditional medicine had failed. Therefore, due to his benevolence and love for people, he decided to offer free treatments. Dr. Usui felt good that he was serving his community selflessly. But as time went by, he started feeling that something was wrong. His healing had started losing its impact. People started taking his advice casually. On introspection, he realised that it was because his treatment was freely available, people were taking it for granted. So he summoned his disciples and instructed them to discontinue free sessions. 'Neither should you charge them exorbitantly, nor should you treat for free, but ask for a minimum fee. Let people pay for what you are giving them'.

"His sudden change in attitude was criticised by people. But Dr. Usui did not pay heed. People were now paying a price for what they were getting, and so they listened to him sincerely. They implemented his suggestions seriously and as time went by, there was a marked improvement in their health. Dr. Usui's systems were an overwhelming success.

"Till date," Harry continued, "you will never find a Reiki teacher who heals without consideration. It is Dr. Usui's strict instruction that Reiki should not be given free of cost. In India, we have a similar concept — Gurudakshina — the Guru insists on being paid for the knowledge that he shares with a student. And it is not because the Guru is selfish, but because if he starts giving it out for nothing, then the disciple will never learn what he is supposed to. Somewhere it has to pinch him, only then will the student focus.

"One of my entrepreneur friends is the owner of an industrial house. He has put in his blood and sweat in creating his empire. Having started from scratch, he knows the value of every rupee that he has earned and therefore he takes his financial decisions judicially. But, his son is a drug-addict and a womaniser. When he comes to office the only thing he does is throw his weight around and abuse juniors. And his behaviour is not surprising. He has earned the CEO's position free of cost. It was his inheritance and so he has no idea of the 'responsibility' that comes along with 'authority'.

"You will be surprised to know that both Mukesh and Anil

Ambani started their careers in Reliance on the floor. They weren't bestowed with 'free executive positions' from Day One. Both brothers have worked their way to the top due to their own competency. And that is why they are so tough. Although their father is no more, the sons continue to scale new heights."

"Harry, you said we must not give free lunches," I interrupted, "does that mean we must not do charity? There are so many people out there who are unable to support themselves, who will take care of them?"

Initially, I was apprehensive about asking him this question because I thought he might not like someone challenging his words, yet I just had to be brave enough to ask.

"Dave," he replied patiently, "there is nothing wrong in charity. But it must be an empowering process, it can't be just spoon-feeding. If you spoon-feed people, they have free resources without any increase in their competency. So there is no growth. The moment you stop giving them charity, they are back to Square One. Only if your support is directed towards empowering them and increasing their competency, will they become powerful in the process.

"Have you noticed how a young child learns to ride a bicycle? His father helps him for a few days. The father runs behind the cycle, holding on to the seat or the handle, while the child strives to maintain his balance while pedalling forward. But one day the father has to let go. He knows his child will fall down a few times and also hurt himself. But that is the only way by which he will get better and learn how to balance.

"Imagine a situation where the father does not cease his support and 'guarantees' the child that he will be around forever. Surely, the child will not hurt himself, but will remain forever dependent on him. Without his support, he will simply be incapable of advancing. So instead of empowering, his father is only making him dependent. Similarly if you are creating 'special allocations' or 'reservations' to help people, it must be only during the initial phase when they need genuine support. You cannot let it last forever. Like in Sam's case, if the government gives free meals to school kids it is appreciated. At least for the sake of food, their parents will send them to school and the little ones will get knowledge. But, if the state plans to support them throughout their academic careers and beyond, then it certainly requires a change in strategy.

"Take the case of public sector departments. The employees know that they are permanent and cannot be fired. This leads to a great deal of complacency. They become lazy and lethargic at work. Efficiency is low and the desire to upgrade is virtually missing. At the back of their mind they know that whether they work efficiently or not, their employment is guaranteed. So why bother?"

At this point, I felt that Harry wanted to say something more. But was stopping himself. As a businessman, he couldn't afford to be politically incorrect. However, he was keen that we should get his message and therefore he was telling us about nature's maxim — the survival of the fittest. To remain fit one has to constantly change and evolve with circumstances. It's a simple rule, either you perform, or you perish. Unfortunately, the communist mind does not understand this. It promises free lunches to people without checking their competency. The masses feel that the state is giving them a great boon by assuring employment. But, in reality this is a destructive policy. In the long run, the whole economic system will be under the threat of collapsing. This is exactly what happened in the former USSR.

"When Sameer was in school," Harry was saying, "he was extremely fond of Robin Hood. 'What a nice fellow he is,' Sameer used to tell me, 'he loots the rich and gives money to the poor'.

"I was shocked when I heard this. No Bania can tolerate such words. I could forgive Sameer for considering that Robin Hood was a nice fellow, because he was a kid then. But there are many people who believe that the rich must donate their wealth to the poor so that economic inequality can be eliminated. I would be happy if this was true, but unfortunately it is not so. Unless people learn the dynamics of handling wealth, it is virtually impossible for them to break the vicious circle of poverty.

"Dave," he said looking directly at me, "please don't get me wrong. I don't intend to sound like an arrogant miser. I sincerely believe that wealth must be shared for the benefit of our community. One of these days we will discuss how wealth has a miraculous tendency of multiplying when circulated. Om Group spends more than Rs 20 million every year on its Corporate Social Responsibility programme. That is by no means a small amount. But our projects our intended towards *empowering people to empower themselves. We don't believe in pampering at the cost of evolution.*

"As far as your question is concerned," Harry said while looking at Sam, "by seeking free allocations from the state, people are disempowering themselves. So they are at a loss, not the state.

"A long time ago, the Parsee community had to leave Persia unexpectedly. They left all their property and assets behind, in their homeland, and boarded ships and set sail for India. When they came to this country, they had no possessions with them. But, they never asked the government for any special favours or privileges. Against all odds they worked hard to regain their fortunes. And in the process became powerful creators of wealth. You will be surprised to know that at one point in time, four of the top ten richest corporate houses in India were created by Parsees. This included the Tatas, Shaporji Pallonji Group, Godrej Group, and the Wadias. The Parsees are a very small community. They are less than one lakh in all, yet they commanded four of the top ten positions. What a phenomenal achievement!

"Take the case of the Sindhis. After Partition, they also had to leave behind all their assets and properties in Sindh and migrate to India. They had faced tremendous losses. Yet, they never asked the government for any special quotas. They struggled and within a couple of decades recreated their fortunes. Today, we all know that the Sindhis, in general, are a wealthy lot. Those who seek free allocations may not like to accept the fact, but there is no substitute for evolution."

I looked at Sam. He seemed both happy and impressed with the answer. Harry stepped down from the stage and started walking down the aisle between chairs.

"I will tell you a beautiful story before we wind up for today. One day a little boy found a caterpillar in his school garden and brought it home. He was so overjoyed with his new discovery that he showed it to all his family members. 'Keep it carefully in a jar,' his father advised. 'And put some plants inside for the little one to eat.' The boy did as he was told. Every day he watched the caterpillar and brought it new plants to eat.

"One day the caterpillar started behaving strangely. The boy was worried, seeing his pet struggle like this. He quickly summoned his father who understood that the caterpillar was creating a cocoon. He explained to his son how a caterpillar turns to a butterfly.

"The boy was excited when he heard this. He waited for days to watch the transformation happen.

"One fine morning he observed a small opening in the cocoon. The caterpillar was struggling to come out. The boy observed keenly as the caterpillar continued to struggle desperately. For many minutes it strived to break free, but it seemed to be a futile effort. Seeing his pet in pain again, the boy decided to help. He snipped open the cocoon and made the hole bigger. The butterfly emerged!

"But the boy was disheartened when he saw the butterfly. It had a swollen body and underdeveloped wings. He waited for the creature to flap its wings and fly around the jar, but alas, it never happened.

"The butterfly spent the rest of its life crawling around, handicapped because of its crooked body. It was never able to fly.

"Instead of helping, the boy had only harmed the butterfly. Later, his father explained that by intervening, the boy had prevented the caterpillar from pumping blood into its veins which would have developed the wings. Without the struggle, the butterfly's growth was stunted and it would never be able to fly.

"Sometimes challenges are exactly what we need in life to advance further. Now we have two options, either to seek being pampered and cripple ourselves, or to embrace evolution, evolve our competencies, and become powerful in the process.

"The choice is entirely ours."

———

NO ONE CAN PRODUCE GREAT RESULTS WHO IS
NOT THOROUGHLY SINCERE IN DEALING WITH
HIMSELF

—JAMES LOWELL

"Are you alright?" Abhi asked, placing a consoling hand on my shoulder.

Today's session with Harry was over and people were walking out of the auditorium. Yet, I was sitting in my chair, eyes closed and deep in thought.

"Yes, I am fine," I replied. "You carry on. I will join you in some time."

"All right then," Abhi said, patted my shoulders and left.

I took a deep breath and looked around me. The whole world had frozen in time. The empty chairs, the podium, the screen. Everything was still.

I slowly flipped through the pages and went through Harry's words. The experience I had today had shattered a lot of long-held beliefs. His words had touched the deepest core of my heart.

'As long as you are getting wealth by hacking it, you will never focus on enhancing your Being. For the sake of petty benefits you will confine your whole existence.' Harry's words echoed in my mind. In between them I could see the dim reality of my life.

I had always considered myself to be a creative genius who could innovatively tap into the company's cash flow, but now I realised how this narrow attitude had affected my competency.

I was already 27, but hardly had any savings of my own. In the last two years I had changed four jobs. Without any sense of purpose or direction, I was just drifting around. Work was a compulsion and perhaps that was the reason why everything about office really sucked. Be it the HR training, getting into crowded trains every morning, or interacting with my boss. I hated it all.

Sitting in the auditorium that day and deeply sunk in gloomy thoughts, I resolved to leave my past behind. Enough is enough, I said to myself. I don't want to spend the rest of my career chasing trivial issues. I want to break free of the mediocrity and experience a great life.

Little did I know that was exactly what was planned for us in the coming days.

GIGANTISM — THE THINK BIG APPROACH

On the third day there was a lot of hustle and bustle in the auditorium. Strange faces had started becoming familiar, and striking up a conversation with fellow participants was now easy.

"Hi, I am Raju, HR Manager of Silicon Technologies," the gentleman sitting beside me said and extended his hand.

"Nice meeting you, Raju," I smiled. "I am Dave from Om Group."

"Oh, so you work in Harry's company. That's great. So how has the training been so far?"

"Oh, it has been very enlightening."

"I have wanted to do this course since a long time," Raju said. "I have heard excellent feedback from participants from previous batches."

"Really?"

"Yes. After attending this course, corporates have found that their sales have skyrocketed, professionals have found their incomes have zoomed upwards, and young entrepreneurs have taken off on their dream ventures."

"Wow!" I exclaimed.

"Yes, the demand for this course is so high that currently there is a two-month waiting period for people who are not part of Om Group. I had applied two months back, only to get a seat in this month's course."

Just then Harry walked in and Raju and I decided to talk later.

Immediately, Harry began, "Yesterday, we saw how our Being or Competency is essential for success. Today, we will focus on the second circle, 'Doing'. Doing is equally critical because without actions, all competencies are futile. What is the use of our abilities and potential, if we don't express them?

"During the next phase of this course we will align ourselves to the 'GATE' model that I have developed after an in depth study of the life of some great entrepreneurs. It is a very powerful model that we have adopted at Om Group and you can adopt it in your personal lives too."

Harry turned to the projector. The word 'GATE' had appeared on the screen.

G – Gigantism

A – Aggression

T – Trust

E – Efficiency

"The word GATE is an acronym. It stands for 'Gigantism', 'Aggression', 'Trust', and 'Efficiency'. Of what I have learnt from biographies of great entrepreneurs, these four elements can be the pillars of any organisation's success. If any one of them is missing, you cannot achieve explosive growth."

"In the next four sessions, we will study each element in sequence. We will first discuss some inspiring incidents from Ambani's life and then I will give you a plan of action which you can follow for yourself.

"Let us begin with the first element. For any entrepreneur, and the Banias in general, gigantism implies doing things in outrageous proportions. It means doing things at the highest scale, massive levels of production, and working in huge setups. It is about focusing on being the biggest, rather than an 'also ran'.

"Way back in 1966, while setting up his first factory, Dhirubhai had to send people from his Naroda factory to Germany to study their technology. At that time, barring Reliance, all other manufacturers were using outdated Indian machinery. So there was a dearth of people who could handle sophisticated machinery. Just a day before their departure, one of his managers asked him, 'Is there anything specific you want us to keep in mind?'

"Dhirubhai put his arm around the manager's shoulder and asked him if he had heard of the Tatas and Birlas.

"The man responded positively. 'Yes, I have heard of them.'

They are the two biggest industrialists in India.'

"'And that is the only thing I want you to keep in mind,' Dhirubhai said. 'While you are there, keep repeating to yourself that one day we have to be bigger than Tata and Birla. But, we can be bigger than them only if we master our machines. Just don't limit yourself to handling the machines we need. Go with an open mind. Keep your eyes open. Demand to see everything, look into everything, and learn everything. Make note of all that they are doing, planning, developing.'

"'They will not tell you everything by themselves. You will need to ask them, needle them for answers, and pester them. Be after their life. What you learn will depend on what questions you ask. Don't be with them for just the scheduled six hours in a day. Stay in the mill for 24 hours. If necessary, sleep there. And most importantly, make friends while you are there. We need to have friends everywhere, if we have to grow big.'

"That was how he used to think," Harry continued as he closed the red diary.

"Even before setting up his first factory he had already decided that he was going to beat the Tatas and Birlas. And he never felt any shame or hesitation in declaring his dreams. 'Don't be afraid of mockery,' he would say. 'Go ahead and align people to your vision. It is not your individual journey, the whole organisation is supposed to move along with you. And how can you expect them to move forward unless they know what they have set out for?'

'"When we went out for our evening walk, we would pass the Burmah Shell Refinery where he had worked,' Dhirubhai's wife Kokilaben told me once, 'and every time we passed it, he said that one day he would own a similar refinery. At first, I thought he was just trying to impress me, but there was such ferocious determination in his eyes, that you couldn't help but believe it would come true'.

Harry told us that 'Gigantism' was one quality that separated Dhirubhai from his peers. Whatever he would set his mind to do, he would do it in a scale unimaginable by most of us. He had one simple mantra for his team at Reliance and it was *'Think Big, Think Fast, and Think Ahead'*.

"In the 1970s, a leading newspaper carried a story about Reliance's Think Tank. It comprised highly talented people who were paid for just one skill — sensing opportunities. Their job was to assimilate critical information and news from all corners of the world and try to sense any potential for generating revenues! Dhirubhai had given them strict instructions that no opportunity should go unnoticed. He wanted to be the first one to pounce on anything worth striving for. 'And also keep track of the most talented people in our industry,' he advised them, 'even talent shouldn't go unnoticed because *talent lost is opportunity lost*'.

"A leading business journalist has mentioned in his memoirs that Ambani's decisions were clearly an outcome of his 'Think Big' approach. 'While other businessmen preferred hiring cheap labour to save costs, or just hired the bare minimum number of employees to keep operations running, this man was forging ahead and hiring the best people just to track opportunities for him! Is there any wonder then that in a few years this man owns the country's biggest company? It has to be him!' the journalist wrote.

"Ambani's information sources were so well-connected, that he knew exactly what was going on in business, politics, and bureaucracy, at any given point of time. At times, he had more information about a competitor than a senior executive in that company. And it was not that he had ample cash for availing of such extra comforts. Even then, cash flows were stringent. But his vision and foresight were beyond such concerns. 'No compromise on Gigantism,' he would say."

Harry recollected how as a young Bania, he had heard his elders say, *'Nishan chook maaf, nahi nichu nishan'*. It simply meant that 'one could be forgiven for missing the target, but not if he aimed low'.

"It was the same case with Dhirubhai. After the success of his Naroda refinery, Dhirubhai chalked out some very big plans for Reliance. He wanted to foray into polyester on a massive scale. But, the problem was that banks weren't interested in funding his ventures. The scale at which Dhirubhai was planning to conduct his operations was mind-boggling. Bank managers found his vision and plans too massive to approve. For days, Dhirubhai personally met the top bosses of various banks and tried to convince them. But, all of them refused outright. So he was in a fix. On one hand, he didn't have enough personal finances to fuel his ventures and on the other hand, banks had shut their doors. Many colleagues and friends advised Dhirubhai to cut down the size of his mammoth project to something that would be accepted by the banks. They reasoned that it was better to get a small project approved rather than getting nothing at all. But Dhirubhai wasn't ready to compromise so easily. *'Mediocrity is like quicksand. Once you are trapped in it, it's virtually impossible to come out,'* he argued.

"And so having realised that traditional ways of getting funds were unavailable, Dhirubhai decided to launch an Initial Public Offering and accept funds from the general public. 'If the banks don't want to lend me money, no problem, I will seek money from the common man!' he declared. And as the proverb goes, 'fortune favours the brave'. He got a tremendous response from the people. I will elaborate this when we discuss the 'Trust' element of the GATE model, but do you know how many shareholders Reliance had?"

"Three million," someone said loudly.

"Yes. During Dhirubhai's tenure, Reliance had more than 3.7 million shareholders. It was a world record, which stands unbroken by any other company. And like his gigantic projects, he booked gigantic football fields and cricket stadiums for his Annual General Meetings. And even these were too small. During the meetings, thousands of shareholders would line up for hours just to get a glimpse of him.

"I really want you to get this," Harry said. "Whatever you do again and again becomes a habit. So, if you think mediocre thoughts all the time, then you will develop the habit of mediocrity. Whatever you do will be mediocre. However, if your thoughts are gigantic, then gigantism will become a habit! And whenever anything reaches the level of habit, it achieves perfection. Because then, even though you may not be conscious about it, it will happen on its own.

"The same thing happened with Dhirubhai. For years, he programmed himself to play the big game. Day in and day out he would chalk out enormous plans for Reliance. If you spent an hour with him, you would hear words like 'Outrageous', 'Large', 'Exorbitant', 'Exponential' at least a dozen times. And he wasn't doing it consciously. Over a period of time, these words and the thought behind them became an unconscious habit. And then the miracle happened. He developed the Midas touch and whatever he touched became gigantic. Be it manufacturing, sales, public relations, finance, human resources, or even advertising.

Whatever he touched, became big."

"Harry, we find that all companies are slowly growing and evolving," a girl asked. "The normal rate of growth is around 10 percent. And yet there have been times where Reliance galloped at a mind-boggling rate of 400 percent per annum. How was Ambani able to raise the company to such massive heights and in such a short span of time?"

"Riya," Harry replied after glancing at her name tag, "you might find it difficult to believe this, but there were times when Reliance galloped at the rate of 1100 percent per annum. And this was not a temporary phase, it lasted for a fairly decent period. Within 40 years, Dhirubhai was able to create an empire of US$ 16 billion. And even after he died, the growth has not stopped. His sons Mukesh and Anil have increased their respective market capitalisation multiple times. Taken collectively, the Ambani family is one of the richest in the world. Obviously, when such statistics are presented one wonders how they were able to achieve it. But before I delve into that discussion, I would like to narrate an incident from my personal life.

"During his high school years, my son Sameer had a passion for cricket. Every evening when I returned from office, he would tell me about his recent batting achievements. 'Dad, I scored a century today', or 'Dad, I hit three sixes in an over', he would boast. Being his father I took pride in his accomplishments.

"One day, however, he returned home quite dejected. He hadn't been selected for his school cricket team. I tried to cheer him up, but the incident seemed to have had a profound impact on him. Next day, I went to his school and asked his coach why he hadn't been selected, despite his strong record.

"'Look there,' the coach pointed at a corner of the school ground. 'That's Sameer with the kids he plays cricket with.'

"I followed his gaze and was surprised. Sameer was playing with kids half his age and size!"

"'Mr. Shah,' the coach said, 'your son who is in the ninth grade, is playing with third and fourth grade kids. No wonder he scores so many 50s and 100s. Ask him to play with the senior kids and he runs away!'

"'And why does he behave like that?' I asked.

"'It's quite simple Mr. Shah. He is so obsessed with winning that he plays only those games which guarantee him success. If he plays with the senior kids, there is a fear of losing or getting out quickly. This will shatter his ego and his illusion of greatness which he pleasantly holds on to. So he chooses to play small games.'

"I could not help but agree with his coach. His observation was bang on target.

"By the way, we all live like that," Harry drew our attention towards the board. "Look at this circle."

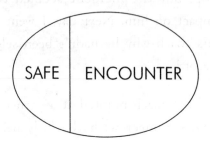

"The figure is divided into two parts. One is the 'Safe Zone' and the other is the 'Encounter Zone'. We have all unconsciously divided our life into these two zones. In the Safe Zone, we have placed those activities which we are comfortable doing. And in the Encounter Zone are those activities which we find difficult and hence resist doing them. Like in Sameer's case, playing with young kids was in his Safe Zone, but playing with seniors was in his Encounter Zone. Therefore, consciously or unconsciously, he avoided it. But, if you introspect, you will notice *all 'growth' happens only when you step out of your Safe Zone and encounter a new activity.*

"Remember the first time you learnt how to swim. Initially, there was a lot of resistance when you encountered the water, but you put the fear of failure aside, stepped out of your Safe Zone and jumped into the water. And once you learnt how to swim, swimming became a part of your Safe Zone. This is how we all move ahead in life. We constantly encounter new activities that begin by being in our Encounter Zone, we master it and it gets pushed into our Safe Zones. This is how we learn foreign languages, sports, dances, virtually everything in life. But it is very easy to do this when we are young kids. As adults we are so conscious of our ego and public opinion that the fear of failure prevents us from learning anything new. Once we achieve mastery over a certain activity we simply repeat it for the rest of our lives to avoid failure.

"So coming back to the question Riya asked me, the reason why companies like Reliance rise to such meteoric levels is their continuous insistence on stepping out of their Safe Zone and encounter something new and challenging. When Dhirubhai was at a senior executive position in Yemen, he decided to quit his 'safe, secure job' and venture into business. At that time, he had a one-year-old son and his wife was expecting their second child. For a married man with such responsibilities, it is perhaps the most difficult time to quit job and start his own business. There was so much expected from him that he could hardly afford to take any risk. Yet, he not only left his job, but also the country, and came back to India. His decision was strongly opposed by senior family members, but he was deaf to their criticism and started his business in Mumbai. Initially, as an importer and exporter of commodities he was doing well for himself and had no need to change his line of business, yet, when he saw the opportunity in yarn trading, he ceased his commodities business and ventured into yarn trading. His decision raised suspicions as yarn trade was considered to be extremely risky and was dominated by big players in the industry but Dhirubhai was unfazed. Again in the yarn trading business, he was making good profits but he felt he could earn more if he started his own production unit. Against all odds, without any technical knowledge and with a totally raw group of people, he built a synthetic fibre factory at Naroda. And from manufacturing synthetic fabrics at Naroda to polyester at Patalganga to naptha at Hazira and Petroleum at Jamnagar, he constructed one gigantic plant after another. These weren't small setups, they were mammoth structures spread over hundreds of acres of land fully equipped with the latest technology.

"'Whenever you sense an opportunity,' he advised me on the foundation day of Om Group, 'You must seize it. Even if it involves encountering the toughest challenges to achieve your dream. Never, ever, ever, freeze yourself at one level. Always ask yourself — what next, what next, what next?'

"I too have been asking myself the same question for the last 40 years," Harry confessed. "After every successful venture, I did not stop to rest, but asked myself 'What next?' Om Enterprises which was established in a rented garage has today become Om Group, a corporate giant making over a billion dollars in revenue every year."

A huge round of applause greeted his words.

"Gigantism is the outcome of ceaselessly encountering bigger, higher, and tougher goals. After every accomplishment, you don't become complacent but decide to take up something even mightier. Each gigantic challenge you confront, may either give you success or failure, but will make you a more powerful human being."

"Haribhai, what if someone stays in his Safe Zone forever, what's wrong with that?" an old man asked. "I have owned a small retail shop for the last 27 years, and I am a happy man."

"Is that you Ram?" Harry asked.

"Yes," the man answered.

"Oh, Ram is an old friend," Harry told us. "He owns a retail outlet close to our headquarters."

"Ram, you may have the privilege of being happy at one level," Harry said. "But, public traded companies cannot do just this much. They have to show consistent growth to attract investors."

"Yes, but I am not a public limited company," Ram argued.

"Yes, my dear friend, I am fully aware that you are not. But, if you are big you enjoy economies of scale which give you a competitive edge. If an organised retail chain opens a store here, they will offer huge discounts to customers, which you will not be able to afford, and, God forbid, you may be forced to shut down your store. I am not scaring you, but these things have happened in the past. Don't we know of how Walmart threatened the survival of thousands of small retailers in USA?"

"But that is not the case currently! And I am totally safe," Ram countered.

Harry looked at Ram for a long time, perhaps he realised that Ram was unnecessarily holding on to his opinion. But, Harry wouldn't give up so easily.

"Ram, *ships are safer at the harbour, but that isn't their purpose.* Look at this slide," Harry opened a new presentation. "This illustration is from the story of the *Samudramanthan* or 'the churning of the oceans' from Indian mythology.

"One day, the Gods decided to extract hidden treasures from the deepest recesses of the ocean. They wanted to consume these secret treasures to increase their powers. But there was a problem. These treasures couldn't be taken out easily. They could only be extracted by 'churning the waters' when equal force was applied from both sides. The combined strength of the Gods was required at one end. But then, who would occupy the other? Many suggestions were made, but they all proved to be futile. Ultimately it was decided to approach the Demons. The Gods hated asking the Demons to join them, but it was necessary to have a strong force on the other side, so that the treasures could be taken out.

"On the appointed day, the Gods and Demons took up their positions, and the churning began. One by one the secret treasures started emerging. First, came the Goddess of Wealth, then came the wish-fulfilling being. As they continued churning, all the hidden treasures started surfacing.

"Unfortunately, for many years the western world has laughed at the Hindus for believing in such an illogical story. But it has a deeper meaning. The story mustn't be taken literally, it is just a metaphor.

"The divine beings are all of us, the demons symbolise challenges, and the hidden treasures in the ocean are our hidden potential. What the story conveys is that within each one of us there are many hidden talents. We are all blessed with the power to fulfil all our wishes, create infinite wealth, and other such gifts. But these powers cannot be acquired by just summoning them. It is only when we confront one mighty opposition after another do they gradually surface and express themselves.

"So, you may choose not to play tough games," Harry told Ram, "it's all right. At least 99 percent people in the world choose not to. Once they freeze in a certain comfort zone they just grow in tiny proportions. But then they will not realise the powers that lie at their disposal. It's like having electricity in your house, but choosing to live in darkness.

"I always ask participants at my seminar to think beyond

the mundane and focus on doing something big, really big. If you are a doctor, ask yourself, why not start a pharmaceutical company? If you are teacher, ask yourself, why not start your own chain of coaching classes or even a university? If you are a computer engineer, ask yourself, why not own an IT company? Dhirubhai used to tell his team over and over again, do not focus on creating another local company, instead focus on being a global player. Do not stop when you cross Rs 10 million in revenue, instead expand your vision to earn ten times more than that, or perhaps hundred times that amount."

"Harry, what about the fear of failure?" a participant asked. "There have been so many times when I have wanted to attempt new things, but the fear of not making it always haunts me."

"Shift your focus from 'success' to 'growth'. When you are hell bent on being successful, you will subconsciously take up small tasks because it is easy to fulfil them. Even Sameer did the same thing in school. But when your focus is on 'growth' you will willingly take up big challenges in life. *A man who seeks growth knows that if he succeeds, his confidence will increase, but if he fails, his experience will increase.* So, either way he has an advantage.

"When Dhirubhai was asked to choose a slogan for Reliance, he chose — Growth is Life. His justification was, 'For me, growth is life. As long as I live, I grow. There is no limit to one's growth. At Reliance, we continuously revise our vision and set up new targets and goals to achieve.' We all know the miracles that he created. Take a look at this slide, it plots Dhirubhai's achievements from the start to the end of his career."

Filled petrol at a petrol pump	Owned the world's biggest grass root petroleum refinery
Came to Mumbai with just two sets of clothes	Within 25 years became the country's largest garment manufacturer
Started with a capital of Rs. 15,000	Ended with a market capitalisation of Rs. 65,000 crore
Started in a 150 sq. ft. rented office	Became one of the country's biggest private land owners.
Started with two employees	Had 85,000 employees by the time he died
Failed to pass Class 10 exams	Was awarded an honorary MBA from the world's biggest universities

"Isn't it unbelievable," Harry said, "that a poor, barely educated villager, without any contacts, support, or resources could create the world's biggest and richest corporate empire?"

"Is it true?" I asked Abhi.

"What?"

"That the Reliance group is the world's biggest and richest?"

"Well, the market capitalisation keeps fluctuating because of stock movements, but yes, recently there was an article in the newspapers which claimed that collectively, the Ambani brothers have beaten the Walmart heirs to become the world's richest heirs."

"All right then," Harry looked around, "do you have any more questions? Because I still have to discuss the steps to achieve gigantism."

Nobody raised their hand.

"Good," Harry said after waiting for a few moments. "Let us now discuss the steps to take towards gigantism. I suggest you take down the main points for your reference."

Abhi created a new presentation on his laptop. I was taking down every word as well as I could.

"Take a look at this slide here," he said.

(1) Identify the Right Waves

(2) Work with Giants

(3) Give Up to Go Up

"The first and foremost step towards gigantism is to identify the right waves. Dhirubhai did it with polyester. While other traders were still stuck dealing in cotton fabrics, he could foresee that the polyester wave would sweep the economy soon. There were many other waves, or, in other words, opportunities, but polyester seemed to have a huge potential. Reliance capitalised on it and achieved gigantic growth. Azim Premji's success story is similar. His company Wipro had always been manufacturing soaps and oils, but Premji spotted the opportunity in Information Technology, seized the wave, and ventured into it boldly. Within the first few years itself, Wipro's revenues touched the roof. In fact, all those associated with the IT wave grew phenomenally; Infosys, Tata Consultancy Services, Google, Microsoft, Yahoo, and others.

"When the telecom boom swept the world, all leading corporate houses such as the Tatas, Birlas, Ambanis, and Ruias, got into it. Why? Because the telecom wave had tremendous potential for growth and profits. Even the new kid on the block, Sunil Bharati Mittal, rode the telecom wave and became one of India's richest men. In Mexico, Carlos Slim capitalised on the telecom wave and made such enormous profits that he was once said to be the world's richest man. Another good example is that of the retail wave. Kishore Biyani, of Pantaloons fame, was originally concerned with manufacturing readymade garments, but he foresaw the organised retail wave and exploited it earlier than most others. The success of the Big Bazaar chain of stores has increased his market capitalisation well beyond people's wildest imaginations.

"So, the first step towards gigantism is to identify the right wave. If you are not a corporate, but an independent businessman, or professional, then you must look at the waves in your industry. If there is an entry-barrier for the big waves, then try to identify small segments or niche areas from where you can begin. Just remember the old dictum — To be rich, be where the money is — because money fuels growth.

"The second element of gigantism, is that in order to be gigantic you have to work with giants. Gigantic-minded people have a different charisma altogether. There is a vision and grandeur in their style of working, and of course, ability. When such people align with your cause, it empowers you tremendously. When most other mill owners in India were working with domestic companies, Dhirubhai decided he would import machinery from technology giant Du Pont in Germany. The fibre for the polyester was imported from the reputed Asahi Corporation in Japan. Working with international companies meant taking care of co-ordination and other issues. 'But only they have the ability to execute what we plan on paper', Dhirubhai justified.

"As Reliance grew, Dhirubhai hired more and more top executives from public sector organisations. Traditionally, public sector employees were considered sluggish. But, Dhirubhai insisted on hiring them. 'The massive projects I am envisioning have not built by any other company before. Only the government of India has been involved in such projects. So, I need top government executives, because only they have the acumen and ability to handle huge ventures', he explained."

Harry told us that there are two types of people in the world. The first type includes people who are scared of doing something big, and the second type comprises people who are inspired by something big. To fuel your growth you need to hire people from the second category. They are rare, expensive, and dictatorial in their way of working, but they are worth their weight in gold.

Harry narrated an incident that took place in the Naroda factory. At that time, Dhirubhai had no experience in setting up a textile mill. It was a completely new venture for him. Amongst his team members, there was only one engineer and a couple of matriculates. The others had not even passed their eighth grade exams. But they were all gigantic-minded, ambitious youngsters. They had an indomitable spirit and wanted to do something different, something challenging, and exciting. None of them had either the qualifications or the experience, but they were fuelled with the passion to do something exceptional.

One journalist asked Dhirubhai if the project was even viable, considering the plan was to build a world-class factory with the help of such raw youngsters. But Dhirubhai justified his decision, 'If Lord Ram could win Lanka with the aid of an army of monkeys, why can't I build my factory with the help of my team. Aren't they better than monkeys?'

"And they did build a wonderful factory!" Harry's eyes were shining. "In fact, a World Bank survey of 24 leading textile mills in India found that only the Reliance factory had been developed as per world standards, all the others were lagging far behind.

"People often argue, 'After we build a gigantic company we will hire gigantic-minded people. Why waste big money on them now?' But the truth is that gigantic-minded people create gigantic organisations. Big people pave the way for big results.

"So, my advice to all of you would be to recruit people not only on the basis of their knowledge and experience, but also check whether they have the motivation, the inspiration to do something phenomenal. Such people will really multiply our growth.

"Did you notice?" I asked Abhi, "although he has officially retired from Om Group he still keeps on thinking about the company's progress."

"Yes," Abhi smiled, "after all, he, too, is a Bania!"

"You bet!" I agreed.

Harry took a breather. And after that continued, "Next, we come to the third step which says that you must 'Give up to go up'. Although the phrase sounds like a cliché, it has a direct relationship to gigantism. The more you implement it, the faster you will scale greater heights. I was studying the history of some of the world's major corporations, including Reliance, and it was interesting to note that in most cases the promoters did not take out the profits and dividends in early years, but ploughed it back into the company for its growth. The more they 'gave up' on personal withdrawals the more it provided fuel for the company's growth. And it is not an easy thing to do; when you have your first big bucks there are lots of personal luxuries you want for yourself. But postponing wisely, will only reap richer rewards."

"Next, one must give up authority and decision-making. People love to treat their projects as their own babies. Like a mother cannot part with her baby, some people cannot part with their projects. But, HELLO," he shouted, "this is the corporate world. There is no place for sentiments here. We must all learn to give up the 'I' in our tasks and learn to delegate authority and decision-making to worthy people. If you insist on controlling everything, you may manage the project better, but you will restrict growth."

Harry added a word of caution. The thoughts of gigantism and mightiness could be hallucinatory. At times people got lost in their dreams and forgot to check ground realities. Dhirubhai always said, 'Dream, but dream with your eyes wide open'. Don't get carried away by dreams and illusions because its implications will be directly proportional to the orbit in which you revolve. *In a gigantic orbit, even the smallest mistake will have gigantic implications.*

"Well, with that we come to the end of today's session. Tomorrow, I will tell you a very exciting story of how a Chinese military general and his small troop did the most unbelievable thing to defeat a large army. But, for that you will have to wait."

"He does this intentionally," Abhi complained to me. "He always gives you a little glimpse of what will follow the next day so that we eagerly wait for his lecture."

"Yes, now even I am curious about what the general did."

"But today, I will tell you something else that is very interesting," Harry was saying.

"If you ever happen to visit a zoo, observe carefully the enclosure where the elephant is. You will be surprised to find that this gigantic creature is actually tied to a wooden post with nothing more than a weak-looking chain. Considering the mighty strength of the animal, he should easily be able to break free, shouldn't he? But he does not even try. You know why?"

Nobody knew.

"It's because when it is a baby, it is tied to a strong tree with a strong chain. The baby is weak, but the chain and tree are strong. Not being habituated to being tied up all day, it tries desperately to tug and pull at the chain and free itself, but in vain. One day it accepts that all the tugging and pulling won't help it at all. It stops trying, and stands still. Now it is conditioned to being tied up.

"The zoo keeper is aware of the creature's behaviour and so when the baby elephant becomes a giant, he can be tied with a weak rope to a small post. It could, with one tug, walk away free, but it goes nowhere, because it has been conditioned! Somewhere, deep down in its mind, the elephant knows that any attempt to break free is futile and therefore never attempts it. A gigantic creature with tremendous power has now become a victim of its circumstance.

"Most of our behaviour is also a result of conditioning," Harry said. "It becomes a habit. As young children we dream of conquering the world and reaching out for the sky. We have gigantic plans and ambitions. But, a few failures in our life, and we are convinced that we are powerless against our circumstance. Our own beliefs limit our growth.

"My invitation to you is that from today keep all your past memories of failures aside," he pleaded. "Our essential nature is one of tremendous power and potential. Each one of us is born a 'giant', we just have to realise our true worth!"

———

WHERE THERE IS NO VISION, THE PEOPLE PERISH
—PROVERBS 29: 18

An 'eye opener' took place later that day.

We had just reached our dorms after the session and Saloni called us up. Harry wanted to check on the status of our assignments.

We rushed to his office right away only to find him deep in conversation with someone. They were poring over a big chart that had been spread out on the table. After a few moments, Harry saw us and asked the man to excuse him. He called us inside.

"Did you get your notes with you?" he asked.

"Yes, we did."

"May I have a look at it?" he asked.

I gave him my notebook while Abhi switched on his laptop and opened the presentation he had been working on.

There was silence in the room. Harry was absorbed in our work. I happened to glance at the chart on his table. On the top left corner were the words 'VISION 2020' and below taking up most of the space was a planner, featuring every month from the current month till 2020. Already several notes had been made in most of the months on the chart. I nudged Abhi gently and gestured that he should look at the chart.

Harry spoke after a few minutes, "Excellent work, boys! This is much better than what I had expected."

"You liked it?" I asked in disbelief. I thought he would point out at least a dozen mistakes.

"Yes, you have written it in a narrative style. That makes it a very interesting read."

"And the presentations?" Abhi asked.

"Yes, they are looking good too. In fact, just a few minutes back I was telling Mr. Nair," he introduced us to the man still seated near the table, "that the corporate culture is all about creating a legacy. Tomorrow, if I am not there, the show must still go on. You guys will take this project forward and reach out to more people."

Mr. Nair nodded and smiled at us.

"Tell me," he asked us, "what was the topic of discussion today?"

"Gigantism," I answered.

"Correct. Now consider a gigantic company like Om Group which I created over four decades. Tomorrow, if I die, do you think the company will shut down?

"Far from it!" he hit the arm of his chair with a sudden rush of energy. "Today, Haribhai Shah has become irrelevant to Om Group. I have created enough leaders to ensure that the show does not stop after I go. Even in my absence the company will continue to scale greater heights.

"Look here," he pointed to the chart on his table. "It says VISION 2020. The vice-presidents of our different undertakings have created a plan for the company covering the next decade. Sameer and I weren't even present at the meeting. It is only now when Mr. Nair showed it to me that I have become aware of it."

I sulked at Harry's words. This man was preparing a plan till 2020, and here I was stuck between deciding what to do a half hour from now!

"But, what if someone is unable to find worthy successors?" Abhi asked.

"That is no excuse, Abhi. Worthy successors are to be spotted, groomed, and empowered over a period of time. That is exactly what I am doing with Dave and you," he said. "**A leader who cannot create worthy successors is not fit to be a leader in the first place.**"

"Write this down, Dave," he said pushing my book back to me. "I had told you about the three elements of gigantism. Please write down the fourth one."

I started writing. What Harry said that evening was difficult to digest immediately. It was only later that night when I read it again, and again, did I realise how priceless his wisdom was.

"Gigantism cannot sustain without effective legacy. True leadership lies in empowering your people to grow without you. Even in your absence the show must go on with equal efficiency. **The vision must outlive the visionary!**"

AGGRESSION – THE UNSTOPPABLE FACTOR

The next day began with Harry introducing us to a group of management students who had flown from London to attend the training session. Their professor had heard about the course and wanted to find out what was being taught. After the introductions, Harry started with the second element of the GATE model — Aggression.

"When the earthquake hit Saroon, everything crumbled to dust within seconds. Seeing the pitiable condition of the residents, many different organisations, including the local police, NGOs, political parties, social service groups, the army, and others, came forward to help. Although each group tried its best to help people rehabilitate, none of them were as effective as the Rapid Action Force."

Harry showed us pictures of the RAF troops. They were dressed in light blue uniforms.

"Can anyone tell me why the Rapid Action Force was more effective than any of the other groups?" Harry asked.

"Because, as their name suggests, they were quick and aggressive," a participant said.

"Yes."

"And they were continuously engaged in some kind of action," another ventured.

"Absolutely correct," Harry seemed impressed.

"In fact, after a natural calamity or a great disaster, it is always the armed forces that are summoned. They are always 'raring to go' and accomplish the task with speed and courage. As corporate houses we need to learn a lesson from them. More often than not we create unnecessary red tape that gives priority to needless formalities, so growth takes a back seat," Harry pointed out.

The slide on the screen changed. The word 'Aggression' appeared in big letters.

"The second element of the GATE model is 'Aggression'. It has three components — Speed, Risk, and Unstoppable. We will study them in sequence."

The foreign students were sitting right beside us in the first row. We offered them some writing material so they could take notes.

"Speed is one virtue which is grossly lacking in our lives," Harry began. "Unlike the Rapid Action Force which is always on its toes, we are dangerously slow in our execution of plans. Part of it is because of our laziness and part of it is because we are conditioned to lead a slow life.

"I will give you a classic example. When we were in school we all learnt the story of the hare and the tortoise. We were told that when the race started the hare was leading, but because of his complacency he went to sleep. The tortoise pursued the hare even though it was slow and eventually overcame the hare to win the race. And the story ended with the moral — Slow and steady wins the race.

"This is the perfect example of how society conditions us in the wrong manner. Since his or her early days, the child is made to believe that 'slow and steady wins the race'. This is an incorrect conclusion. The moral of the story ought to be 'If you sleep when you are speeding, you lose out'. The emphasis should have been on being unstoppable rather than anything else.

"Tell me," he asked us, "how many of you have seen an Olympic race, or any other race for that matter, where the slow and steady runner won?"

No one had.

"So, if none of us believe in this then why the hell do we follow this bullshit and teach it to our children in schools?" he shouted. "Why the hell do we programme ourselves to be so cautious?"

There was pin-drop silence in the auditorium. I had never seen him so angry before.

"Rather than teaching our children to be fast and swift in executing their plans, we teach them to be 'slow and steady'. It is we who condition them to avoid risks, be cautious, and keep walking on the well-trodden path. These rules are fine, but they all lead to mediocrity. The outcome will be nothing that is more than average."

After a few moments, Harry had calmed down enough to start talking again, "The other day I was reading an interview with Sunil Bharti Mittal, India's fourth richest man. Mittal says that 'in business, speed counts more than detailed analysis'. I couldn't agree more. When Mukesh Ambani was asked what was Dhirubhai's most striking characteristic, he said it was an 'infectious impatience'. Dhirubhai was an extremely impatient man. Once a project was approved he would get extremely restless till it was finally executed.

"I too have tried to emulate this characteristic. The construction guys who work with Om group call me 'Hurry-Bhai'," he laughed.

"And I can't blame them for that! I am extremely particular about the deadline and achieving targets on time. My team knows that if they overshoot the deadline, they're dead. I will grill them so intensely that they would never again dare to lag behind in the work schedule. Not that I'd like to be another Hitler," Harry explained, "but so much is at stake that we cannot afford cost overruns due to delayed projects."

When Harry compared himself to Hitler, it reminded me of Deepak Patel, my boss in the Mumbai office. I had almost forgotten about him after coming to Saroon. Though I must admit, now that I had 'got the shift', he didn't appear as bad as I had thought he was.

"Out there in the corporate world you will find many types of people. Some people prioritise discussions. They will have meetings and more meetings and spend hours discussing every single topic. Whenever an issue pops up, they will meet. When another issue pops up, they will meet again. For long periods of time, talks, opinions, and arguments will flow but when it's time to take some concrete action, they will pass the buck.

"Some people are plan-oriented. They have lots of ideas and concepts in their mind. Whenever you meet them, you will always find them planning and thinking and dreaming, and conceptualising, but they are either lazy or incompetent when it comes to actualise these plans.

"I have met many such 'big talkers'. During our meetings they make tall claims but when it's time to get the ball rolling they keep on postponing indefinitely. Mr. Rai, our vice president, sarcastically calls them the 'work in progress' people. Whenever you call them to check the status of an assignment, they are always in a 'still doing' mode. Days, weeks and months will pass but they will still tell you, 'Yes, I am doing it', 'Yes, I am working on it'. But nothing concrete shows up.

"When you call them to check on the status of a pending assignment, either the desk attendant would have forgotten all about it, or the assistant would be ill, or the manager would be out of town.

"So, when I say, 'speedy execution', I mean giving the highest priority to the final result. Discussing, planning, strategising, and talking, is all okay, but ultimately results must show and that too, on time.

"Dhirubhai used to always tell us that speedy execution counts more than cost savings. Once, when his Naroda factory needed some spare parts for the imported machines, Dhirubhai had them flown from Germany on priority. Then, he realised that no transport trucks would be available to get the parts from Mumbai airport to Ahmedabad since the transporters were on strike. So, he purchased two trucks in Mumbai, one to carry the parts and one as backup, and he received the consignment. The trucks were later sold in Ahmedabad.

"Any other businessman would have felt helpless and cursed the government, or blamed the transport unions and made himself a victim of circumstance, but not a great businessman like Ambani. To him it didn't matter whether the transport strike would last one day or three days, or at what price the trucks could be resold. These were secondary concerns. The only thing that mattered was quick and ceaseless execution of plans at the factory."

Harry said that there were times when Dhirubhai was so quick in getting results that he could beat you in your own game and that too without compromising on project quality. Relaince's Patalganga plant was created in eighteen months. Richard Chinman, then the director of Du Pont was awestruck. He admitted that to construct a similar plant in USA would have taken at least 26 months.

"It wasn't just that one time that they baffled Du Pont. In 1989, an overflowing river close to the factory caused extensive damage to Reliance's chemical complex. More than 50,000 tonnes of silt and floating junk seeped into the complex and submerged most of the areas close to the complex. Technical experts were flown in from Du Pont and they estimated a minimum of 100 days before the complex could be operational again. This meant production would stop for more than three months. Reliance's manufacturing team told Du Pont experts that they needed at least two huge compressors ready in 14 days. The Du Pont guys laughed and mocked them, 'Out of two, if you can get even one compressor ready in one month, you will be lucky'.

"Guess what?" Harry said, pausing for maximum effect, "Reliance had both compressors ready in 13 days, one day before their planned schedule and the whole complex operational in just 21 days, more than 79 days before Du Pont's estimation!

"Later, Mr. Malhotra, head of manufacturing unit explained, 'If Du Pont tells us it will take 100 days, then we know they haven't quantified the task properly, because only by accident can they arrive at such a nice round number. We assessed the requirement precisely and worked like the Rapid Action Force'."

Harry told us that Blitzkrieg was the central philosophy in Dhirubhai's life. Once, he inaugurated more than 100 Vimal fabric stores in a single day. Banking on 'speedy execution' he achieved in 40 years what Tata and Birla took three generations to accomplish.

"At Om Group we have a simple philosophy. We always approve tenders based on the supplier's ability to deliver on time. Cost, although crucial, is a secondary factor because if one thing is delayed, everything is delayed, including revenue. To save a penny we will end up postponing a pound."

The London students were listening to Harry attentively. They seemed to be totally absorbed in the lecture. Harry asked if we had understood the first element correctly. We nodded and he proceeded.

"Next, we come to the second element of Aggression – 'Risk/Daring'.

"A few years ago, my friend's son asked him for some money. He said he wanted to invest in the stock market. Initially, the father refused and told his son that he should focus on their own business rather than play around with stocks. But, the boy insisted and ultimately his father had to give in. He reluctantly gave him a small sum of Rs 10,000 and a dozen warnings and threats, 'It is my hard earned money. Don't you dare lose it at any cost'. Unfortunately, it so happened that the stock the boy purchased, crashed in the market. His father grilled him intensely when he came to know of the loss. The boy was so shocked with the experience that since then he has never invested in stocks. Originally, only the father was risk averse. Now, even the son became risk averse. And when the son's son grows up, he too will be kept away from the market. This is how beliefs are imprinted and inherited through generations. They will never be able to leverage from a wonderful platform called the stock market.

"Had the story been about a Bania businessman, he would have told his son, 'You want 10,000 bucks. Here, take them. Play with the market. If you make gains, it's great but if you lose, no problem. Consider the 10,000 bucks as the price paid for learning the market dynamics.'

"Now, what that father would have done was to give freedom to his child to play with stocks. He is encouraging him to speculate fearlessly. And guess what, in most cases the son will end up multiplying the father's wealth. This is how the Gujaratis and Marwaris raise their children. Their fathers are gutsy risk-takers and encourage their children to do the same. And it is precisely this fearless attitude that has made these two communities the richest in this country. For decades they have dominated and continue to dominate the stock market.

"At times, the conditioning we receive in childhood is so strong that it is difficult for us to bet our money on risky ventures. Consciously or subconsciously, we all try to live in our comfort zones and stay away from anything big and risky. However, if you observe the wealthiest people in the world, you will see that they had an amazing appetite for risk and had a bias for all ventures big and mighty.

"There is a story from Ambani's life that is not so well-known. Dhirubhai's first business venture was in partnership with one Mr. Chambaklal Damani. It was a joint venture and both were equal partners. But, there was a stark difference in their style of working. Damani was a very cautious businessman. He was averse to speculation and avoided risky deals. Ambani, on the other hand, was outrageous and daring. If his gut-feeling was strong, he would seize a risky opportunity with both hands. Once, Ambani invested a huge amount of money in yarn. He was expecting a price rise and wanted to earn profits by holding on to the stocks. When Mr. Damani came to know of this, he was angry. He insisted that the stock be sold off immediately. Dhirubhai tried to negotiate, but Damani wouldn't budge. So Ambani sold the stock, but he had secretly sold it to himself using the name of a third party!

A few days later, yarn prices increased significantly. Ambani's prediction turned out to be true. He made enormous profits.

"The next day he called up Damani and said, 'I am ready to share the profits with you, but you must promise not to interfere with my decisions in the future.' But, it is said that it was extremely difficult for Damani to give up his conservative style of working, and therefore in time Ambani decided to dissolve the partnership. Though both were equal partners once, Ambani's insistence on taking bold decisions made him a global phenomenon. As far as Damani is concerned, little was ever heard about him after that."

"Harry, what if someone takes no risk and just plays safe?" Robin, a participant from the London group, asked.

"It is purely his choice, Robin" Harry replied. "But remember this," he walked towards the white board and wrote — *If you are not taking any risk you are taking the biggest risk*

"What does that mean?" Robin asked.

"If you remain status quo, there is the risk of becoming obsolete, the risk of becoming stagnant and the most dangerous risk of becoming predictable."

"Predictable?"

"Yes, because if you don't do anything unexpected, your competitors can easily guess your next step and make their plans. Only if you do something beyond their expectations can you catch them unawares.

"I will give you an example. When Dhirubhai was constructing a polyester filament yarn plant, he was told that the annual countrywide consumption of the filament was 6000 tonnes, not more. Yet Ambani created a plant with an initial output of 10,000 tonnes per annum. His competitors said it was a wrong move and the unnecessary surplus production was to go waste. Even Dhirubhai wasn't sure, but he had a gut-feeling that the market would expand and absorb the surplus capacity. He ventured boldly and sure enough the plan did work. The economies of scale created through higher production brought down the conversion cost making it more affordable to customers and the entire lot was sold. Dhirubhai's detractors, as always, could do nothing but remain mere spectators.

"In 1994, Reliance's conversion cost of yarn was 18 cents per pound, as compared to Western Europe's 34 cents, and North America's 29 cents. And the best part was that Du Pont which had initially sold this technology to Ambani was now importing the yarn back from him!"

"Unbelievable," Robin exulted.

"Yes, it is indeed unbelievable. Dhirubhai was a failure at math in school, but in business his calculations were razor sharp."

"He was a failure in math?"

"Yes, he failed in math when he was in tenth grade, due to which he had to repeat a whole year in school. In fact, quite a few successful businessmen have been dropouts. Bill Gates was a dropout, Steve Jobs was a dropout, Richard Branson was a dropout. All these people couldn't complete formal education but became highly successful businessmen.

"Peter McColough, former chairman of Xerox made the same point about his Harvard Business School class of 1949. He said that, 'the record of accomplishment corresponds negatively with the standing in the class'. The top people did not do that well. The middle third did. The guys who got the highest marks tended to be in the middle when it came to accomplishments.

"Interesting, isn't it?" Harry asked. "That the so-called intelligent students in school ended up being 'mediocre' in life, but the average performers overtook them and made it big.

"Do you all agree with me, folks?" Harry raised his hand expectantly. "That the B-graders and C-graders, more often than not beat the A-graders in the real game of life."

Yes, I said to myself. Recently, during my school alumni meet, I was surprised to learn that some of the 'naughty backbenchers' were making more money than the ace students from our batch.

"And do you know why this happens?" Harry started walking back to the board, "because of this," he wrote twice – Daring.

"The intelligent school child is conditioned to be very disciplined and obedient all through childhood. He is expected to always be on his best behaviour, never rebel, misbehave, or break rules in school. He is expected to sit in the first bench and do exactly what the teacher says. Simply put, his entire environment pushes him to be a 'conformist'. So when we grows up, he continues to hold this 'conformist' mentality and prefers having a secure job, shuns from risky investments and is very precautious in his decisions.

"On the other hand, the occasionally naughty and mischievous kid has a little 'rebel' hidden in him or her. They will dare to disobey the system, question everything you tell them, climb high walls, and hang upside down from trees in the park. In other words, they are never afraid to challenge the system or go against a conformist mentality. Quite naturally, when they grow up it is easy for them to venture on untrodden paths. And that is what business requires! We need daring, nonconformist, rebellious people to change society.

"When Dhirubhai decided to make 10,000 tonnes per annum of PFY, instead of 6000 tonnes, he was taking a big risk, but that was how he always was.

"Do you know Dhirubhai once swam in shark infested waters just to win an ice-cream!"

"Huh ?" I blurted to myself, "still unsure of what I had just heard."

"One of his old friends from Aden narrated to me this story." Harry elaborated. "Dhirubhai was aboard a ship with his friends when he overheard someone announcing a bet — 'whosoever swims to the shore will win an ice-cream'.

"The statement was perhaps uttered casually since the deep waters around the Gulf of Aden are generally shark infested and there had been a few attacks too. But the next thing his friends saw was Dhirubhai had already taken a splash.

"He swam half a mile to the shore and joyfully accepted the ice-cream!"

"Why such desperation?" someone asked.

"No, it was not desperation." Haribhai overruled. "It was the sheer thrill of adventure that excited him. This unusual adventure did not go unnoticed and Ambani became popular as the one who *swam with sharks for an ice-cream*. In another instance he lead a rebel campaign against the Nawab of Junagadh because the people of Junagadh in Gujarat wanted to join India and not Pakistan. It was no wonder when he plunged into business and challenged every license restriction that the government imposed on him. Other businessmen would willingly confine their growth within the permissions given by the government, but people like Dhirubhai would fight back, and win.

"At times it pays when you dare to be different," Harry pointed out. "When Colonel Sanders launched Kentucky Fried Chicken, he was 62 years old. People advised him to retire, because they thought he was too old to start a business. When Frederick Smith of Fedex promised an overnight delivery service, people thought he had gone nuts. When Dhirubhai said he would make a phone call cheaper than a postcard, and when Ratan Tata said he would make a family car that would cost only $2000, industry experts scoffed at them. But these guys were daring, they took risks and succeeded in their ventures!

"I would like to share a few thought-provoking words that I once read. *If we do what everybody does, we will get what everybody gets. But if we want something that no one has, we need to do something that no one does!*"

"Human beings are strange," he continued. "We want extraordinary outputs by putting in ordinary efforts. It seldom works that way. If you want something extraordinary, you need to do something extraordinary, isn't it Robin?"

"Yes, it is," Robin smiled.

"Are you satisfied with the explanation?" Harry asked.

Robin nodded and his friends smiled at Harry.

"Great, then let's move on to the last part of the day! The third element of 'Aggression' says, 'Be Unstoppable'!

"I have studied the biographies of many successful people. The one thing they all had in common was their ability to generate victory despite extremely unfavourable circumstances. Each one of them, when confronted by challenges, would soar high to combat them instead of giving up or submission.

"In his early days as a commodity exporter in Mumbai, Dhirubhai once received a strange enquiry from a Gulf trader. He wanted a huge quantity of manure mixed top-soil for use in the garden of a rich sheikh. It was a big order and the payment was high, but nobody had ever before executed such a deal.

"All of us advised Dhirubhai to ignore the order as the requirement was huge and the time given was too little. But that was the sort of challenge that spurred him on. He asked for an additional premium payment over and above the offered price and the Gulf trader agreed.

"The very next day, Dhirubhai sent all of us to several slums in Mumbai and we got together all the jobless youngsters we could find. Then, he asked them all to fan out, all over the city, and collect all the dung they could find. The youngsters were surprised by our demand. They had done many odd jobs, but collecting dung was weird. But, Dhirubhai was offering them good money, so they didn't refuse.

"An agricultural science specialist was hired to look after the preparation of manure. Heaps of dung was collected, processed, packed, and shipped to the trader before the stipulated time. Dhirubhai made really big money with the deal. But apart from the money, what I am trying to highlight is the 'never say die' attitude. If there was an opportunity to make money, it had to be tapped. Even if it involved making money from a weird thing like manure."

"Harry, some people naturally have a 'never say die' kind of attitude," Abhi pointed out, "but how can we develop such an attitude in our lives?"

"That's a very good question!" Harry nodded. "How can one develop such an attitude?

"You will require two things. First, you must destroy all backup plans and safety nets that you may have created for yourself. Has anybody read *The Art of War* by Sun Tzu?"

Just two or three people raised their hand.

"Sun Tzu describes a very interesting incident in his book. Very long ago, a Chinese military commander was ordered to crush an invading army. The commander set out with his troops but on entering the enemy's territory he realised that he was hugely outnumbered. So he did a very unusual thing. He instructed his subordinates to burn all the boats in which they had arrived!

"And then turning towards his soldiers, he said, 'The boats in which we arrived were our only hope of going back. Now I have burnt them, so there is no possible way of going back home. The only option we have is to win this war and capture the enemy's fleet to go back. However, we are hugely outnumbered and so we will have to put up our best fight.'

"And to cut a long story short," Harry said, "on realising that they had no option but to defeat the enemy, the Chinese soldiers fought with such ferociousness and courage that the enemy was completely crushed!

"On any other day, they would have put up an average performance. But having realised that this was a 'do or die' situation they fought with extraordinary zeal and bravery. By 'burning the escape boats', the general ensured that his small group of men was able to defeat a big army.

"So you mean we must destroy all safety nets?" Abhi asked.

"No. I am not against safety nets. I am only against over dependence on them! Usually, we tend to create a backup for everything. But, the awareness of a safety cushion often kills our passion to go full steam ahead with our main project. Thus, one must give minimum importance to backup plans."

"Okay, so the first part is to 'burn our escape boats' and the second part?" someone asked.

"The second part is to 'toss your hat over the wall'!"

"Toss your what?" the young man behind me blurted out.

"Toss your hat over the wall!" Harry raised his voice gleefully.

"When a certain American president was a young boy, he used to loiter around with his friends in the fields of Texas. Once while walking with a friend, they came across a high brick wall. The young lads decided to climb the wall and go to the other side. But the boys were too small and the wall was too big. After a few attempts, the young president gave up.

"He conceded defeat and decided to go back. But as soon as he turned around to walk away, his friend did the most unexpected thing. He removed the young president's hat and tossed it over the wall. The young president was shocked and screamed at his friend. But the friend replied, 'It is now confirmed that somehow you will go to the other side of the wall. Now your hat is at stake, so I am sure you will go there for it.'

"And, the president somehow managed to climb the wall

and get back his hat. Years later, he wrote in his autobiography that his young friend taught him an important lesson about success, *'When something precious is at stake, nothing can stop us from achieving it. So to inspire oneself to action one must intentionally put something at stake.'*

"In real life too you will observe the same thing," Harry pointed out, "most entrepreneurs play the normal game of growth. They follow the formula,

$$\text{Inflow} - \text{Outflow} = \text{Profit}$$

"From their total revenue inflow, they deduct the total cost outflow and the remaining amount is their profit. It is a safe game but offers minimal growth. If, one wants to achieve extraordinary growth, then they will have to apply the reverse formula,

$$-\text{Outflow} + \text{Inflow} = \text{Profit}$$

"First he has to divert his outflows towards a plan or a project, and then wait till that investment gives him positive inflows.

"The reverse formula involves higher risks, because in the earlier formula you are only giving away money from your accrued earnings, but in the reverse formula you are giving away your money first. Metaphorically speaking, 'you are tossing your hat over the wall'!

"And since your own money, or maybe your borrowed

funds, are at stake, it is confirmed that you will go out of your way to ensure that you are not only able to recover it, but also get profits in return.

"Look at the track record of any successful company and you will see that at some point in its history, the promoters put their hard-earned money at stake and plunged ahead with risks. That is the only way by which you can move towards a higher orbit. If you play the straight formula of 'inflow less outflow equals profit' you will only have marginal growth.

"So, what are the two factors?" Harry asked Abhi to revise the key concepts.

"First, we must minimise our dependence on backup plans."

"Hmm. And second?"

"We must have something at stake in the process."

"Correct. If you have this dual combination, nothing in life can stop you from achieving anything."

Harry told us that unless a 'do or die' situation confronts us, we never act on anything. He knew many people who often complained that they wanted to work on their fitness but had no time to go to the gym. Interestingly, just a minor heart attack and those people would have all the time required to go to the gym and attend yoga and aerobics classes and so on.

"If you observe human history carefully, you will realise that most countries became superpowers after they had been through a war. Technically, it sounds strange. Wars are supposed to destroy you, not make you prosperous. But, the truth is exactly the opposite. War creates so much destruction that the whole country has no option but to involve itself fully in rebuilding the nation. It's a 'do or die' situation. And when people have no option but to move ahead, they will do so.

"The First World War completely destroyed Germany and Italy. Moreover, the destructive 'Treaty of Versailles' was imposed on them to ensure that they never became powerful again. But to the world's surprise, within two decades, both Germany and Italy became military and technological superpowers. Germany became so strong that it conquered large parts of Europe.

"The same phenomenon was observed during the Second World War. All eight countries that had participated in the war, namely USA, UK, France, Germany, Italy, Spain, Russia, and Japan, suffered substantial destruction. By 1945, when the war was over, five of these eight nations had literally collapsed. But within ten years, these same eight countries became the most powerful nations of the world! From the bottom to the top, in less than one decade. Look at Japan. After two nuclear bombs, the world had virtually ruled out all possibilities of Japan standing on its feet again. But in less than a decade, Japan stunned the world by its meteoric rise!

"War destroys all your backup plans and puts everything that you have at stake. Hence, in the post-war period the whole civilisation has no option, but to bounce back with double strength.

"Andy Green, the chairman of Intel Corporation once said, 'Only the paranoid survive'. At Om Group too, we hate complacency. Instead we invite challenges and competition. At times, so much is at stake that we have no alternative but to emerge as winners. But that's the fun of it, isn't it?"

Despite his age and rapidly deteriorating health, Harry spoke with so much passion that it made your heart beat faster just hearing him.

"Tomorrow, I will tell you how one single inappropriate action destroyed one of the world's biggest organisations. From boasting of 85,000 employees across the globe, they were reduced to merely 200 employees. But I would like to end today's session with a story from the life of King Shivaji, a seventeenth century ruler of western India.

"On the outskirts of Pune, a city in India, is a fort called 'Lion's Fort'. The fort is named in memory of a brave warrior named Tanaji Malusare.

"Tanaji was a military commander in King Shivaji's army. History says that while Tanaji was at his son's wedding, he received urgent summons to capture the fort atop a mountain which had come under the enemy's possession. Tanaji left his son's wedding and quickly collected his men to attack the enemy and recapture the fort.

"At nightfall, Tanaji decided to climb the mountain using ropes. They chose the most difficult terrain as the enemy would least expect that. On reaching the top, Tanaji ordered his men to cut all the ropes they had used so there was no way of going back.

"His juniors advised him against it, but the mighty courageous Tanaji knew better. And as you must have guessed by now, having no other option but to win the war, Tanaji's warriors put on their best possible fight. By early next morning the fort was recaptured.

"Remember, *at times, people don't perform when you give them a better option. They perform when there is no other option!*"

———

EVERY BODY WILL REMAIN IN A STATE OF REST
UNLESS COMPELLED BY AN EXTERNAL FORCE TO
CHANGE ITS STATE OF REST.

—NEWTON'S LAW OF MOTION

The session was over and I was about to pack my books and pens when Harry made an unexpected announcement.

"Ladies and gentlemen, may I have your attention for a moment."

The participants, who had all stood up ready to leave the auditorium, turned around to look at Harry.

"I want Abhi and Dave to join me here, please."

Most of the participants still hadn't been introduced to each other. They looked around to guess who Abhi and Dave were.

I looked at Abhi in surprise, he was shocked as well. Without wasting a second, we started walking towards Harry.

"What is this all about?" I asked Abhi softly as we passed by the participants.

"I don't know!"

"Welcome boys," Harry said as we climbed up a couple of steps to stand on the stage.

"He is Abhi, and this is Dave," Harry introduced us to everyone. "Abhi is a management student from IIM Ahmedabad, and Dave is a mass communications expert. Since this is my last training session, we have selected both of them to continue my legacy. Abhi is designing a training course very similar to this one, and Dave is writing a book based on the secret diary," he lifted the familiar red diary which he carried with him every day.

"Saloni told me that there are many enquiries about our next training session. Many of you want your friends and colleagues to do this course."

"Yes," everyone said.

"But it will take some time as both our young stars," he put an arm around each one of us, "are still being groomed by me. Meanwhile, you can order your copies of the book in advance."

Harry spoke for a few more minutes and explained the vision that he had for passing on the lessons he had learned and how every person in the audience could chip in by spreading this science so it could reach the whole world.

His speech was finally over and as the three of us

were making our way to the exit, I asked Harry politely, "Harry, why did you announce it? We are hardly prepared."

"When something is at stake in the future," he reminded us, "we are powerfully propelled to take action in the present. And so to make you powerfully propelled to take action in the present, I have to put something at stake in the future."

And then he looked at Abhi and me and gave us both a friendly slap on a cheek.

"I tossed your hat over the wall," he grinned like a cheeky Bania and walked away.

TRUST – THE BOND THAT STRENGTHENS

As soon as we entered the auditorium the next day, all the participants wanted to talk to us.

"I want all my employees to attend your training," one entrepreneur told Abhi.

"I want a dozen books for my staff," an exporter told me.

"I need 350 copies," the dean of a business school demanded, "one for each MBA student."

"I want to distribute copies to all my community members," a trustee said. "And I want autographed copies, okay?" he caught hold of my sleeve to get my attention.

Frankly speaking, I was staggered by this newly bestowed celebrity status.

Thankfully, Harry entered the auditorium at the right time and the crowd around us quickly dispersed.

"Gigantism and aggression will help you create a tall structure," he started, "but it requires a strong foundation to support it. Such a rock-solid foundation will be provided by the next two elements, 'Trust' and 'Efficiency'.

"Before I begin, I want to know how many of you have heard of a company called Arthur Andersen?"

"Isn't it the same company that was connected to the Enron scandal?" I asked Abhi.

"Yes. They were accused of shredding essential documents and conducting false audits," he told me.

Not many others seemed to remember much about the company, and so Harry started telling us its history. "Arthur Andersen was one of the world's biggest audit firms. It was founded more than 150 years ago, and in 2001 its annual revenues were more than $9 billion. However, owing to its involvement in the Enron scam, the world lost its 'trust' in Andersen. And guess what happened. Within no time, the whole firm went bankrupt and 85,000 people had to relocate their jobs.

"What is interesting is that on May 2005 the Supreme Court of the United States reversed the conviction charges on Arthur Andersen leaving it free to continue its operations. Officially, it is legal for any client to give business to Arthur Andersen, however, because of its lost reputation, companies are distancing themselves from it. Even its long-standing clients who had enjoyed a long association with the company till the Enron scam was detected, are no longer interested in any association with Andersen. Currently only 200-odd employees operate from Chicago and that too, only to sort out pending legal cases.

"This is what happens when people lose trust in you," Harry said. "Even the biggest corporation can fall overnight."

I was reminded of the Satyam scam and the millions of dollars that investors lost on account of fraudulent practices carried out by the promoters of the company. Once it was evident that there were wrongdoings in the company, within a few weeks, the share price which was pegged at around Rs 500, came tumbling down to less than Rs. 10 on the National Stock Exchange.

"Remember friends," Harry cautioned, "it is easy to cheat or fool someone and gain temporary success, but if we are interested in long-term gains, sustained success will be achieved only if people consider you trustworthy. Today, we shall study the third element of the GATE model — Trust.

"When Dhirubhai was asked to decide on a name for his company, he selected the word 'Reliance' because he wanted the world to know that he was reliable. Back then, Ambani used to export commodities to the Gulf region where Indian businessmen were generally perceived to be unethical and unreliable. Dhirubhai wanted to change that belief. From the very beginning, he insisted on two things — world-class products and punctual delivery. Often, he even incurred losses, but insisted on speedy delivery so that the client's deadline was met. And slowly as time went by, Dhirubhai created a strong reputation for himself in the Gulf markets. 'Rely on Reliance', they used to say.

"Then came the next phase in his career where he wanted to speculate on the fluctuating prices in the yarn market. It was a risky business, but it rewarded well those who understood it. Dhirubhai had knowledge, but no money. Once again the trust he had built up over the years, came to his rescue. He started borrowing loans from relatives, neighbours, and colleagues by telling them, 'If we make profits, we share equally, but if we make losses, I will bear it alone.' It was a tempting deal for the lenders, but they were sceptical at such a generous offer. At times, when you are extra nice, people doubt you!" Harry laughed.

"Despite their scepticism, people started lending him money, but Dhirubhai never made false promises. When he made profits, he shared it with his lenders and when he made losses, he took the whole loss on himself. Once he even went bust, yet he did not cheat the lenders. He borrowed temporary loans from friends to keep the promise he had made. Gradually, the word spread in the small streets of south Mumbai, that Dhirubhai was offering a foolproof deal and money started flowing from everywhere. In the evening, builders, brokers, private financers, and others would line up outside his office to give him money.

"The picture seemed rosy, but Ambani's competitors did not like this at all. They were jealous of his overnight success. The 'outsider' had become a 'reliable man', therefore they decided to play a foul game. Once, when Dhirubhai was out of Mumbai on business, they spread a rumour in the market that he had become insolvent. No sooner had the news start spreading, did anxious lenders start making their way to Dhirubhai's office. At that time the money that he had borrowed had been invested in building up his inventory and he did not have liquid cash with him. Dhirubhai's brothers called him up and suggested that he not return for a while till the situation was brought under control. But, Dhirubhai knew that if he didn't return, the rumour would only scare more lenders. So, the next day he returned to the office and a board was placed outside, 'Rumours of my 'bankruptcy' have been circulated to misguide you. Anybody who wishes to have his money back, is most welcome to do so'. This was a very big risk since he had no money with him, and yet he was inviting his lenders to take their money back. Dhirubhai was confident that if people actually saw him sitting in the office, they would be assured that everything was okay. And guess what! Not a single person asked him to return any money! Dhirubhai's mere presence comforted them.

"Trust is the foundation of any relationship," he said. "The reason why Dhirubhai's 'mega issues' were oversubscribed dozens of times over was because people trusted him. Dhirubhai once joked, 'Normally, people line up outside your office, if you owe them money. But I am lucky, people line up for hours outside my office to give me money!' He also said once, 'We have more than three million shareholders, the highest in the world. And even during controversial times, when fingers were pointed at Reliance and the media asked shareholders to sell our shares, people ignored the analysts and placed their trust in me. Normally shareholders don't like to attend the Annual General Meetings (AGM) of companies, but we have had to hold our AGMs in cricket stadiums and football grounds. Why? Because there are so many people who want to meet me and talk to me. They tell me how they used money from the Reliance shares to educate their children, or pay for their daughter's marriage, or purchased their dream house. Whenever I asked for a rupee, they gave me a dozen.'"

Harry told us that once a leading bank lent a huge sum to Reliance for its petroleum refinery, but when Dhirubhai paid back the loan, the bank felt uncomfortable. As long as the money was with Reliance, the interest from the loan was flowing in consistently and chances of default were minimal. Now the bank would have to re-plan the entire investment. Normally, when you pay back your lender, he should feel relieved, not uncomfortable. But their trust on Dhirubhai was so high that they didn't mind if he continued to be a debtor.

"These days, it has become fashionable to talk about goody-goody things. Look at any beauty pageant like Miss World or Miss Universe and you will see every other model talking about 'world peace' and 'universal brotherhood'. They are trained to give such politically correct answers. Even companies have started training their PR guys to talk about trust, care, respect, and all other nice things to appear media friendly. My only question is how many of these companies actually practise such virtues in turbulent times?

"Very few," he said, answering his own question.

"Ambani was once asked by a journalist, how Reliance has rarely, if ever, experienced any labour unrest or strike at its premises. Unlike other major corporations that have had to deal with strikes in their plants for months, or sometimes even years, Reliance has witnessed the least number of instances of labour unrest. He was quick to reply, 'At Reliance, we have created a legacy of care. And it is not at a superficial level. It is an intrinsic part of our work culture. If an employee's family member is hospitalised, a company car is always available. If any of my retail franchisees is in a financial problem, we encourage him to speak to us so we can assist him. Many of my peers have advised me that I must not mingle with my staff and maintain a distance because of my 'status'. But I don't agree. Just yesterday there was some chaos at our fashion show in New Delhi. I was escorting my guests in the front rows when I was informed that some people were trying to gate-crash. I asked my guests to excuse me and went straight to the entrance. Within a minute I had my sleeves rolled up and joined my team in pacifying the guests. One thing you will never find in me is an unmanageable ego. I want to be like a safety net for my team. Whenever they are in trouble, they can rely on me like an ally.'"

Harry told us that Dhirubhai was the kind of leader who would help you sail through tough times. At Om Group too, he wanted us to exhibit such leadership.

"Trust is not a virtue, but a privilege that we enjoy in people's minds. However it doesn't grow overnight. One has to take concrete steps towards achieving it. In this session, we will discuss three powerful ways by which we can win people's trust.

"First and foremost is to 'honour your word'. Remember the story we all learnt in school? In a far away village there was a shepherd who used to graze his sheep at a nearby hillock. One day, seized by a desire to do something mischievous, he started shouting for help, screaming, 'Wolf! Wolf!'. The anxious villagers came running as fast as they could, carrying sticks. They soon realised that the shepherd was laughing at them. A few days later the shepherd repeated the prank, again the villagers came to help him, but were angry when the young shepherd laughed at them. And one day, when a wolf did attack his flock, the villagers thought the boy was playing a prank on them again, and nobody came to his rescue. This time the wolf ate all his sheep and the shepherd could only cry over his misfortune.

"I can interpret this story in two ways," Harry said, "one is the conventional interpretation that one must 'honour one's word' and 'keep one's promises' so that you win people's trust, because if you keep breaking your promises your customers and clients will avoid you.

"But doesn't that sound like a cliché? We have heard it a thousand times that we must stick to our promises.

Furthermore, saying it all over again makes me feel as if I am leading a moral science class.

"Instead, I am going to offer a new interpretation to this story. According to the science of ontology, 'If you honour your word, your word will honour you'. Let me explain.

"Consider you are the shepherd, and the villagers represent your mind. Interestingly, we all behave like this shepherd in our daily lives.

"Every night before we sleep we instruct our mind to wake us up early next morning for a walk. So, we set an alarm in our cell phones. But next morning, when our mind readies itself for a walk, we press the 'snooze' button in our cell phone and go back to sleep. The next night, once again, we decide to wake up early and when our mind wakes us up, we doze off. If we continue this exercise for a few days, then just like the villagers our mind too reaches a conclusion, that whatever we say is bullshit.

"And then some day, when we actually declare to our mind that we want to achieve a certain goal, it will just not take us seriously. After all we have programmed it to disobey our word!

"On the other hand, if you do exactly what you say, you are programming your mind that you are serious about your declarations. You mean what you say. *And once it is habituated to obeying you, your mind will make positive attempts to 'do' whatever you 'say' to it.*

"Even Mahatma Gandhi has mentioned the same thing in his autobiography. Does anybody know the title of Gandhiji's autobiography?"

"My Experiments With Truth," I shouted.

"Correct. And do you know what Gandhiji's experiment with truth was? He realised that *if he 'did' what he said' then gradually a time came when 'Doing' and 'Saying' became absolutely congruent in his mind.* And then, whatever he said to his mind, it started 'doing' it for him!

"If he told his mind that he wanted to go on a hunger fast for two weeks then his mind would make sure his whole body functioned efficiently without food for four weeks. If he told his mind that he wanted independence for India, the mind would conceive ways by which he could do so.

"Ultimately it's all about mind power," Harry said. "Without the support and *trust* of our minds, we cannot achieve anything. And that is why I insist that people must honour whatever promises they make, especially to their own selves. And I am not saying this because our moral science teacher said so, but because it has been proved scientifically.

"Next time you decide to wake up early and go for a walk, make sure you stick to your commitment. Do it for a few days and your mind will be habituated to 'obey' your commands. And then when you tell your mind that you want to be a millionaire, it will not only honour your word, but will also help you work towards it."

Wow! That was some food for thought, I said to myself. I always had this habit of making promises and then backing out. Could that be the reason why I was never able to seriously achieve any of my targets? Maybe it was true. I really needed to ponder over this one.

"The second element of generating trust is to create emotional deposits. It's a fairly unique concept. Let me try to explain it using everyday parlance.

"We all have a bank account where we regularly deposit and withdraw money. Each time we make a deposit, the balance increases and each time we make a withdrawal, the balance decreases. If you don't have a balance, the bank won't permit withdrawals. For a while it will allow you an overdraft facility, provided you have had a good relationship with them, but if you continue to withdraw more than that, the bank will close your account and cease its relationship with you.

"Quite similarly, whenever you connect with people you unconsciously create a 'relationship account' with them. Every time you do a positive act, like 'fulfilling your promises' or 'delivering on time' you are creating emotional deposits in the relationship account. A few ways of creating emotional deposits would be..." a new slide appeared on the screen, as he said these words.

EMOTIONAL DEPOSITS	
CLIENTS	EMPLOYEES
• Fulfill your promises	• Praise and recognition
• Deliver goods on time	• Good work environment
• Complete tasks accurately	• Listening to suggestions
• Replace defective goods	• Opportunity of growth
• Clear payments	• Promotion/Increments

"And whenever you do something negative such as breaking your promises, or criticising people, you are making an 'emotional withdrawal'. Any act that triggers negative emotions in people's hearts towards you is an emotional withdrawal. They could include any of the following," he said while another slide appeared on the screen.

EMOTIONAL WITHDRAWALS	
CLIENTS	EMPLOYEES
• Breaking your promises	• Criticism and Insults
• Delivering goods late	• Bad work environment
• Incomplete tasks	• Ignoring Suggestions/ Feedback
• Refusal to replace defective goods	• Blocking Growth
• Dishonouring payments	• Demotions/avoiding increments

"When you honour your word, or fulfil your promises, you are creating an 'emotional deposit' in people's hearts. As you continue to fulfil your promises, your deposit starts strengthening and the trust that others have on you, increases. And then once in a while, if you are compelled to break your promise, or in other words, make an emotional withdrawal, people will let you. Why? Because you already have sufficient balance in your account.

"However, the problem with us is that we always tend to make more emotional withdrawals than deposits, and that is why most of our relationships with people are strained.

"We ignore opportunities to praise people, but are quick to pounce on them when they make a mistake. And what happens when you continue to make withdrawals when there is no balance?

"It's simple. People will cease their relationship with you.

"This is what the shepherd did when he cried out for help. The villagers did not trust him anymore, and the boy had created no emotional deposits for them. The first time he fooled them, he was forgiven. They even came to help him a second time. People in our life are generally nice," Harry said, "they provide us with the overdraft facility too! But, when the people were fooled the second time as well, the villagers ceased their relationship with the boy. It was all over. And we know what a terrible price the shepherd had to pay for his pranks.

"One amazing virtue that Dhirubhai Ambani clearly had, was the ability to seize every chance to create 'emotional deposits' in the lives of people around him. This ability went a long way in gaining for him the trust and loyalty of everyone who knew him. Every year he not only promised to declare huge dividends and bonuses, but actually gave more than what people expected.

"Interestingly, during the peak of his career, a leading media group decided to run a hate campaign against Ambani and his organisation. Every day the newspapers carried anti-Ambani and anti-Reliance articles. And this campaign was not small by any means, it was carried out for a subsequently long period of time by one of India's leading media groups.

"Logic says that with so much bad publicity, Reliance's shares ought to have tumbled. But nothing happened. Why? Because Dhirubhai had created massive 'emotional deposits' in the hearts of his shareholders. The bond was so strong that such external issues could hardly break it.

"So my plea to you is, whomsoever you are related do, ensure that your deposits are always more than the withdrawals. Don't be stingy in loving people, or showing then that you care. So, if at times you have to make huge withdrawals, you can conveniently do so without affecting the relationship."

While Harry was talking, I was forced to think of

innumerable incidents in my life where I never bothered to acknowledge the help people had given me, but I had always been eager to criticise them.

"The third element is to give 'win-win deals' to people," Harry continued. "Giving people such deals simply implies that all parties involved in the transaction stand to benefit. No one should be at a disadvantage.

"My tryst with business has lasted 40 years and has taught me that whenever I give profitable deals to people, they start acting fast on it. This helps the whole business chain move smoothly. On the other hand, if people can't see adequate profits in a proposed deal, they will not work enthusiastically towards it. Either they will keep postponing the project, or will try to reduce the quality of their supplies. At Om Group, I have given strict instructions to my purchase managers, 'bargain hard, but don't exploit people'.

"I would like to tell you a real story that is one of my favourites. Many years ago, two young teenagers were pursuing their studies at Stanford University. But they were short on personal finances and they decided to engage the great Ignacy Paderewski for a piano recital. The funds generated from the recital would help them pay for their tuition and hostel expenses.

"The pianist's assistant agreed, provided the boys present a guarantee of US$ 2000. It was a lot of money in those days, but the boys agreed and went ahead with promoting the concert. They worked hard but barely managed to collect $1600. After the concert, the boys gave the pianist $1,600 and a promissory note for $400, explaining that they would earn the amount very soon and send the money to him. It looked like they were in a big mess.

"'No, boys,' replied Paderewski, 'that won't do. I believe in giving win-win deals, not win-lose deals to people. We must benefit from each other's association'.

"Then, tearing the note in two, he returned the money to them. 'Now,' he told them, 'from this $1,600 take all of your expenses and keep 10 percent of the balance for each of you, for your work. Let me have the rest.'

"Many years went by and Europe entered the First World War. Paderewski, who had now become the Premier of Poland, had forgotten about the students. After the war, he was striving to feed thousands of starving people in his country. At this juncture, the only person in the world who could help him was Herbert Hoover, who was in charge of the US Food and Relief Bureau. Paderewski asked for help and Hoover responded quickly, and soon thousands of tonnes of food was sent to Poland. After the crisis was attended to, Paderewski journeyed to Paris to thank Hoover for the relief he had provided.

"'That's all right, Mr. Paderewski,' Hoover replied, 'besides, you don't remember me, but you helped me once when I was a student at college, when I was in trouble. I am only returning the trust and generosity you bestowed on me!'

"Remember," Harry said, bringing the day's session to a close, "whenever you give someone a win-win deal you are creating an emotional deposit in your relationship account with him or her. Sooner or later the good that you do will return to you. Ralph Waldo Emerson says, *It is one of the most beautiful compensations of life that no man can sincerely try to help another, without helping himself!'* "

THE QUALITY OF YOUR LIFE IS THE QUALITY OF YOUR RELATIONSHIPS
—ANTHONY ROBBINS

The seminar was over and as Harry was about to leave a girl rushed up to him.

"Sir, I must confess, your talk on the relationship bank account touched me," she was almost in tears. "Although you spoke about trust in business I think the same logic can be applied in relationships too. Now I realise why most of my relationships are in trouble. I have always taken people for granted without depositing love in my accounts. Now I know where I went wrong."

"You know what?" Harry said, trying to cheer her up, "we all have tonnes of love for people, but it is stocked in the warehouse, the showroom is almost always empty. But, if you want your relationships to succeed, you need to actually express your feelings to people. Let them know what they mean to you. Even a small act of love like buying them a gift, or spending time together, or hugging them creates a strong emotional deposit."

"Sir, but why do relationships feel strained in the first place?" the girl asked.

"It's because after a while, people presume that the love is there and stop making deposits. We take the other person for granted. But, the withdrawals continue.

"People in our life can be very generous. Despite our constant nagging, quarrels, and arguments, they allow us to use the overdraft facility and keep the relationship going. But the real bliss in relationships can only be experienced when there is a surplus balance in the relationship account."

"Thank you so much sir. You have given me much-needed insight," the girl wiped her tears and walked away.

———

That night when I thought about Harry's words I almost drowned under heavy emotions. I realised that it must have been ages since I gave my father a gift, or hugged my mother. Even my relationship with my fiancée was going through tough times. Before today, I had always assumed that other people were responsible for my strained relationships. But that night I realised that I was equally responsible, because I had stopped making emotional deposits.

Thankfully, things were still under control, but a lot had to be done…

EFFICIENCY – THE DECIDING ELEMENT

"A few months ago, Kumar, a technical guy working in our New Delhi office abruptly resigned," Harry began, "his complaint was that in Om Group we marked those who came in late for work; had very strict deadlines; and made people answerable for delayed work; while his friends in another company were getting a much better deal. According to him it was a very employee-friendly company. Their management was 'cool' with people walking in late; did not pressurise them with deadlines; and the quantum of work was relatively low. Kumar quit our office to join that company, and we never heard from him. But six months later he returned, and pleaded with us to re-employ him.

"'But you seemed to be having a jolly good time at the other company,' The HR guy pointed out, 'what happened?'

"'Well,' Kumar hesitated, 'that company went bust.'

Harry flashed a 'I knew it' smile at us.

"Many people complain that we have strict policies at Om Group, and I know that we do. But, it is precisely because of these strict policies that we have a strong foothold in the industry. Even during the recession we have not given a single 'pink slip' to any employee. The so called 'employee-friendly' companies that permitted indiscipline and leniency, have not only shut down, but also rendered all their employees jobless.

"Remember friends," he said, "life is easy for those who set tough standards for themselves, and tough for those who set easy standards for themselves.

"You tell me, which is more employee-friendly, the company that permits casual behaviour and ultimately goes bankrupt leaving the employees jobless, or the one that insists on high standards so that it continues to grow and ensures growth for its people?

"The answer is obvious, isn't it?

"Wherever there is a compromise, there cannot be efficiency. Compromise and efficiency are two diametrically opposite things. At Om Group, we never compromise on the standards that we have set for ourselves. Some people do not like it when we continuously demand higher and better work from them, but that's the way it is. The HR guy told Kumar in clear words, you will have to raise yourself to the level we have set, we will not lower our levels to suit you."

Harry told us that 'Efficiency' was most the critical element of the GATE model. One could do without gigantism or aggression, but efficiency was inevitable. It is the one element that could 'make' or 'break' any organisation, howsoever big or small it is.

"Efficiency is a very wide term. It can include anything and everything under the sun. However, our conversation on efficiency today will include these three elements," he said as a new slide appeared on the screen.

(A) Highest Quality Resources/Standards

(B) Motivated Workforce

(C) Track the Playground

"What is the third point? 'Track the playground'?" Abhi asked me.

"Track the playground..." I looked at the screen trying to guess its meaning. "No idea," I finally said.

"Shall I ask him?"

Harry must have seen a lot of confused faces, because he immediately said, "Some of you will be confused about the last point. But let us finish learning about the first two.

"The first element of efficiency is 'Highest quality resources and standards'.

"When Ambani decided to start a textile unit at Naroda, he had two options: to buy an old mill and renovate it, or borrow money on interest and acquire a new mill. His friends advised him against the second option as it was both risky and expensive. So Ambani asked his staff to look around for an old mill anywhere in Mumbai. Luckily, Gautam Silk Mills, an enterprise run by five brothers jointly was willing to sell off its unit at a price of Rs 3 lakh. Dhirubhai thought the offer was fine and paid a token amount of a few thousand rupees. But on the day of the deal, one brother backed out. 'You keep your old tin with you,' Dhirubhai shot back venomously, 'and even the token amount. Now I am going to go in for a brand new unit, whatever the cost.'

"Later that day, he called for a meeting and said, 'I have decided to buy a brand new mill of our own. Not just a new one, but an absolutely brand new one, with all the best and the latest technology available.'

"Even though he did not have the adequate funds for a new mill," Harry said, "Dhirubhai went ahead with borrowed funds. While the mill was being set up, his brothers would bring brochures of foreign technology providers and try to figure out ways to buy the latest available machinery. They struggled a lot, but never compromised on their insistence for the best quality materials. Quite obviously, in 1975, when a World Bank research team visited 24 mills in India, they declared that only the Reliance refinery was developed as per global standards.

"Whether it was at Naroda, or later at Patalganga, Hazira, or Jamnagar, Ambani always struck to his mantra for best quality resources. In his interviews with the media, he has said that 'At Reliance, whatever we create should be world class. Our work must stand as a benchmark for others.'

"Just yesterday, I was reading an article on Ray Kroc," Harry said, showing us a newspaper clipping, "the founder of McDonalds. Kroc says that at McDonalds they have a zero tolerance policy towards lack of quality. When he started allowing franchisees, Kroc wanted to maintain consistent standards across his entire chain. Implementation was difficult as the concept of franchising was new and the franchisee owners weren't as enthusiastic as Kroc was. While the franchisee was concerned only with his own outlet, Kroc had to look at all overall picture. But instead of lowering his standards to suit the franchisee, Kroc insisted that the highest standards of quality be maintained. He gave them a simple QSVC formula. Each franchisee had to look after four basic elements — Quality, Service, Value, and Cleanliness. Way back in the 1970s, Kroc's staff would go to every franchisee store and inspect the toilets and basins to ensure that there was enough hygiene and cleanliness maintained. Most other store owners only focused on the food without worrying about other things, while some only kept the front store clean, but Kroc had a zero-tolerance policy for every nook and corner of the store. From making burgers to the employee's dress code, and from designing the menu, to the location of the dustbin, Kroc had systematically standardised everything.

"This is what separates world-class companies from the mediocre ones. First, they set the highest standards of quality and excellence and then they stick to it, howsoever dear it may prove to be. *Compromise saves cost but restricts growth.*

"Let me ask you a question," Harry said while stepping off the stage and walking towards us, "which is the most coveted advertisement space on the Internet?"

There was no response.

"I mean, which is the one website or webpage, where, if someone places his advertisement, he is bound to have the highest visibility?"

"It could be the home page of a leading portal," a participant ventured.

"Like?"

"Say MSN, or Yahoo, or Google…"

"Correct! As per Alexa, a web information company, the Google homepage is the world's most viewed webpage and it is every advertiser's dream to put a banner there. But, Google has set a personal standard to keep its homepage free of banners. So deep is their commitment to this, that they have rejected huge amounts from advertisers who wanted to place their banners on the homepage. Many other websites decided to adopt Google's policy but succumbed under fat cheques from advertisers. But, not Google. They stuck to the standard they set for themselves and the policy has worked wonders for them.

Consciously or subconsciously, the human mind chooses to log on to a neat and clean home page as compared to a shabby one.

"So, the first necessary condition of efficiency," Harry reiterated, "is not only to opt for, but to continuously insist for the best."

"Sir, why doesn't this happen in real life?" a man asked, "If it is obvious that a reputed business house should continuously opt for the best quality, how come we see so much of substandard and cheap quality products around us?"

"Well, some people might be lacking the foresight and vision to opt for quality work, but most businesses are struck in a vicious circle. Let me draw a diagram for you," Harry started drawing on the whiteboard behind him.

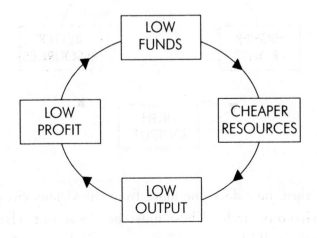

"Most startups face a financial crunch. Since they are starting on a new business, they have limited funds at their disposal. This lack of funds often forces them to opt for cheaper resources, which in turn leads to low outputs, and hence, low profitability. This low profitability further makes fewer funds available. So you see it's a vicious circle!

"On the other hand, established companies like Om Group are in a virtuous orbit. Since they have ample funds they can opt for superior resources, which leads to increased outputs, and hence, higher profitability. This high profitability makes it possible for it to pump more cash into the business."

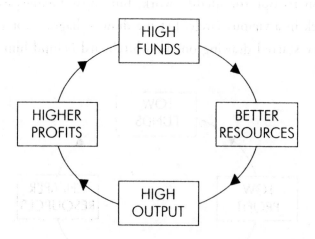

"But then, how does one move from the vicious circle to the virtuous circle? There must be a way out, else all startups would be trapped," someone asked.

"Good question," Harry smiled. "Not only are most startups trapped in the vicious circle, only a few of them are able to break free and move to the virtuous circle.

"The shift from the vicious to the virtuous circle doesn't happen in one go. It happens in many stages. But, to move to any subsequent stage, you need three things — plan, patience, and risk.

"Only when all three elements are present can one break free from the vicious circle. Now, the problem is that very few enterprises have a perfect combination of all three elements working in their favour. Some entrepreneurs have a plan and they are willing to wait for results, but they don't have the guts to take a risk. Some entrepreneurs have a plan and are willing to take risks, but they want overnight results, which is rarely possible, and some people have patience and are willing to risk it, but they don't have a rock-solid idea. Even venture capitalists won't fund the idea if it is not viable. So they are trapped in a vicious circle.

"In Dhirubhai's case that I just mentioned, he had the plan to set up a factory and had the patience to wait till positive results were observed. Now only one thing was missing, to take a risk. He had to borrow funds to buy superior technology. This he did and the results are evident."

Harry felt that the first point of efficiency, was now well-understood, and he moved on to the next point.

"Let's move ahead," he said, "the second point is 'Motivated Workforce'.

"Motivation can do miracles," Harry said. "How many of you watched the first season of the Indian Premier League?"

Almost everyone in the room raised their hand. The mere mention of a cricket tournament was enough to get the audience excited.

"Who was the captain of the Rajasthan Royals team?"

"Shane Warne," we all said together.

"Do you know that the Rajasthan Royals was the most under-rated team at the start of the tournament? They had some of the most inexperienced players and nobody expected them to win. And yet they went ahead and won the championship by beating teams that had many high profile players. What do you think made the difference?"

"Motivation?" a young girl from London guessed.

"Bullseye!" Harry shouted. "A major factor that contributed to their success was Shane Warne and his inspiring leadership. Watch the footage from any match and you will see Shane Warne walking around his team members, screaming encouraging words, clapping his hands, patting players on their back, and pepping them up constantly. Even when players made silly blunders, he would try to cheer them up and get them to focus.

"I am challenging you," Harry said, "take any sport, any game, any tournament played in any part of the world and you will see the winning team had a different level of motivation, a sort of killer instinct to emerge as winners. This attitude makes them super efficient in their work.

"In the first season of IPL, the Deccan Chargers team was led by V. V. S. Laxman. He is a good cricketer, but not a motivating captain. Under his leadership, his team was at the bottom of the points table. But in came Gilchrist as the captain in the second season and the same team emerged as champions. Adam Gilchrist inspired and infused a different level of energy and confidence in the team. *An army of sheep led by a lion can beat an army of lions led by a sheep!*"

Harry told us that 'the personality of the top bosses becomes the work culture of the organisation'. If the top bosses are lazy, the whole organisation becomes lazy. If the top bosses are motivated, the whole organisation feels charged up.

"Can you please tell us how we can motivate people around us?" a management consultant asked.

"Learn to create a place in people's hearts. For only when they have accepted you, will they accept your words,"

Harry said. "The problem with most bosses is that whenever they talk of increasing profits and sales, the employees are thinking 'what a shrewd blood-sucker! He wants to fill his pockets by making us slog'. So whatever the boss says, does not create a stir in people's hearts, instead it falls on deaf ears."

"So what is the way out?" the consultant asked.

"To be authentic."

"Authentic?"

"Yes."

"I didn't get you..."

"Let me explain. During the Indian freedom struggle, many leaders promised to fight for the common man. But their own lifestyle, which was evident by their clothes and mannerisms, indicated that they belonged to the elite. But, Gandhiji was unique. Before asking for the common man's support, he first became a common man. He gave up his rich clothes, and wore a simple loincloth. People saw that he was 'practising what he was preaching' and therefore they were attracted to him. In fact, Gandhi was one of the greatest motivators humanity has ever seen. Imagine convincing people to stand in a queue and be beaten up by British officials, without retaliating. It takes some amazingly high level of influence to generate that kind of acceptance amongst people.

· · · ·

"Take Mandela for example. Before him, many leaders in South Africa spoke against apartheid, but lacked the guts to challenge the government. Nelson Mandela, not only challenged the government, but happily undertook imprisonment fighting for his cause. His selfless sacrifice motivated millions of people to join him in his mission.

"Mother Teresa didn't give sermons on helping the poor. She actually took to the streets of Kolkata treating leprosy patients. No wonder then, hundreds of nuns were motivated by her actions.

"But we don't see such exemplary leadership in the corporate world. About five years ago, I visited a friend who is an entrepreneur. A financial crisis had fallen on his company, and he had summoned an urgent meeting with all his employees. I was in the office when the meeting started. He spoke at length about how employees must show more commitment and dedication at work, but right after the meeting was over, he rushed out to play golf with his friends. No wonder his words failed to stir people."

Harry told us that if we really wanted to motivate people we must first show them that we are committed. Otherwise, all the inspiration will fall on deaf ears.

"In January 1967, the Naroda factory, Dhirubhai's first ever bold venture, commenced operations. However, no sooner had production started, did an unexpected obstacle arise. Some well established manufacturers urged the wholesalers to boycott cloth manufactured by Reliance. They were envious of an upstart entering their exclusive club. The wholesalers couldn't afford to annoy the manufacturers as they were big and powerful. This put Dhirubhai in a fix. On one hand, his factory was continuously rolling out 5,000 meters of cloth every day, and on the other hand, nobody was willing to buy it. He tried every possible way to work through the deadlock, but nothing seemed to materialise. For four months, bales of newly rolled-out fabric kept piling up in the warehouse. More and more working capital was being blocked and the employees were tense.

"The big players thought that Dhirubhai would succumb, pack up, and leave. But, he was not someone who would give up a fight once it had started. 'If we can't beat the wholesalers, we can bypass them and directly approach the retailer!' Dhirubhai suggested, 'There is no way they can stop us from selling directly to the retailer.'

"For the next few days, Dhirubhai's staff met various retailers in Ahmedabad and Mumbai, but the response was lukewarm. Retailers were not used to buying cloth from manufacturers in such a fashion. Dhirubhai observed that the morale of his staff was low. Something drastic had to be done.

"He flew down from Ahmedabad to Mumbai the very next day. On reaching there, he loaded the boot of his old Austin car with bales of Reliance material and drove round the city through the day, from retailer to retailer, hawking his own goods. 'Who can sell my material better than myself?' Dhirubhai said to himself, 'if I can sell it, so can my people'.

"On reaching a retailer's shop, Dhirubhai would place his visiting card on the counter and introduce himself, 'My name is Dhirubhai Ambani. I am a man from the streets, but I want to be big one day. I want you to grow with me, though at the moment I have nothing big to offer you. My brothers, some friends, and I, have just set up a factory at Naroda. We make this knitted fabric there. The wholesalers are boycotting our material because they fear the big mill owners. I offer this material to you. I don't want any money. You sell it. If you make money then give me, otherwise I do not want anything. I am not even asking you for any receipt of goods. I am selling it to you on pure trust. I know my goods are the best and you shall soon be ordering from me soon.' And then he would cheekily smile and say, 'Now, will you not offer me a cup of tea?'

"No retailer had ever seen a young man get out of a car with bales of cloth on his shoulders and introduce himself like that. They had seen many smart, extrovert salesmen, but never anybody so gutsy, so daring, and so straightforward like him. Dhirubhai made rounds for many days in the cloth markets of Mumbai. The shopkeepers were impressed, but cautious at the same time. Many of them thought he was passing them stolen goods. On such occasions, he would show them his factory documents and tell them to call up the factory and check his credentials.

"In a few weeks, sales started picking up. No retailer had ever been offered such lavish terms. Slowly and steadily, Reliance material began moving in the market without any promotion, publicity, or advertising.

"It is true that Dhirubhai succeeded with this approach," Harry said, "but the point I am trying to make is, instead of Dhirubhai relaxing in his air-conditioned office and blaming his sales guys for not generating sales, he took it on himself to hit the road. Company owners are usually status-conscious and don't like selling their own products directly. Even Dhirubhai did not like it. But when he saw that his team was losing motivation, he led from the front. When the staff saw how committed the boss was, it created a natural urge in them to do the same. In the process Reliance was able to create an innovative model of distribution, which was not so popular in those days. The cloth was sold through 1,000 franchisees and in over 20,000 general stores.

"People will only listen to you when they see authenticity in your statements. Unfortunately, most modern bosses are actually opportunists. They use the carrot-and-stick approach to deal with people. And nobody likes being used. Therefore, people retaliate by not performing. When the boss is breaking his head in the office over a crisis, you will find them enjoying solitaire on their computers."

Harry told us that 90 percent of all success and failures could be traced to people's beliefs. He believed that even ordinary people, who had a fire in their belly could achieve extraordinary results. The secret of optimum efficiency lay in continuously motivating and inspiring people to achieve the best. Perhaps that was why John Maxwell, a top coach on leadership, had once said, *'True efficiency can only be achieved when the vision of the leader, becomes the aspiration of the people'*.

"We now come to the last point of efficiency — Track the playground. While the first two points were related to the internal environment, this point is related to the external environment.

"I am using the word 'Playground' because it begins with 'P'. In fact, all the elements in this theory begin with 'P'. I have intentionally used words beginning with the same letter, so that it is easy to remember."

He drew a neat two-by-two table on the whiteboard.

PAISA	POWER
POSITION	PRESTIGE

"Our whole social structure is like a playground," he said, using a pocket laser beam to trace the boundaries of the playground.

"India is a playground. Mumbai is a playground. USA is a playground. The size is immaterial. Any economy or social structure can be a playground and interestingly, whether you like it or not, you will be forced to play on this playground. So, let us understand what this game is, who the players are, what they want, and how one wins!

"All the players in the playground desperately seek these four elements — Paisa, Power, Position, and Prestige. They fight with each other to control these four elements. Paisa is needed because money is an inevitable necessity of life. Power is needed because it helps you get things done. Position is needed because it gives you the ability to issue commands, and Prestige is needed because it gives you social status and recognition.

"These are the four rewards, the lure of which pulls people into the playground. The desire to possess these rewards gives the players ambition. But who are the players? Let us take a look at them, one by one. Interestingly, their names begin with 'P' too.

THE PLAYGROUND

PAISA	POWER	• Politician
		• Press
		• Public Servant
POSITION	PRESTIGE	• Power Broker
		• Priest
		• Page 3
		• Proprietor

"The first and the most dangerous player is the *Politician*. He wants Paisa, Power, Position, as well as Prestige. He has no ethics and no morality. To win rewards he will resort to the dirtiest tactics possible. You have to be extremely cautious of each of his moves because he has no permanent friend or enemy and may switch sides when it is most unexpected.

"The next player is the *Press*. Napoleon Bonaparte once said, 'Four hostile newspapers are to be feared more than a thousand bayonets'. The Press can make you an emperor one day and a pauper the next day. It uses its articles to blackmail people, create, and suppress rumours, each of which you have to tactfully deal with.

"Next in line is the *Public Servant*. This category includes bureaucrats, policemen, tax authorities, the judiciary, staff in public banks, and all the government employees. They are powerful people who control the law and can frame rules and policies that decide your destiny and mine. They can make or break our lives.

"The fourth player is the *Power Broker.* All the underworld guys, anti-social elements, militant groups, and local goons fit in this category. They help politicians suppress the opposition, and are therefore rarely punished. With their men and muscle power, these brokers seek to control the rewards of the Playground. From the Mafia in Italy to the Triads in China, these power brokers work closely with corrupt public servants to run illegal trades and often form 'front companies' to disguise their illegal earnings.

"The fifth player only seems to be a non-entity, but should never be under estimated. He is the *Priest.* The religious priests and spiritual gurus have the ability to make followers behave as per their whims and fantasies. In their battle for power, they can create communal wars, transfer vote-banks to the appropriate politician, and create enough outrage so that their followers will start a revolt. In some places, the priest is himself the politician, which makes the equation even more dangerous.

"Next is your favourite category, the *Page 3* people," Harry smiled. "This includes all socialites, party animals, glamorous people, and superstars — the 'who's who of society'. If the priest can directly influence the masses, the Page 3 people indirectly influence the masses. The common man wants to imitate them in every way. Often the celebrities enjoy a blind fan following, and their statements are ultimatums for their fans.

"And the last and the most critical player, at least from our perspective, is the *Proprietor*. Owners of large business houses, and industrial groups that command the majority of the wealth in any economy are part of this category. They need Paisa for the expansion of their projects, Prestige to attract investors, Power to execute decisions, and Position to command markets.

"Every day as these players play in the Playground, new relationships and equations are created. The Press needs the Proprietor for advertisements, and the Proprietor needs the Press for promotion. The Politician needs the Priest for vote banks and the Power Brokers for harassing opponents. The Power Broker, in turn, needs the Proprietor for cash as protection money. The Proprietor needs the Public Servant for favourable sanctions, and the Public Servant needs Proprietors for corrupt earnings. The Page 3 stars need the Press to become famous, and the Press needs their sleazy pictures to sell their publications. The Politicians need Page 3 superstars to woo the common man during the elections, and the Proprietors need them for brand endorsements.

"In the ultimate game they want to beat each other, but they need each other! So you can see that in any Playground, the direction in which the game moves, or rather the whole society, including all of us, moves, is decided on the basis of the changing equations and relationships amongst these seven players. In Sri Lanka, the LTTE and the government were fighting to acquire power. In Nepal, the Maoists and the royal family were fighting to acquire power. In Sudan, Zimbabwe and many other African countries, powerful rebel groups are fighting each other.

"The common man has a minimal role and merely remains a spectator. The only thing he can do is pick up a newspaper every morning and read about the game's progress.

"In fact, if you look at any newspaper," Harry said, making what I thought was a remarkable observation, "you will find that 50 percent of the news relates to these seven players and the changes they are bringing about in the world, which is nothing but the redistribution of Paisa, Power, Position, and Prestige."

Harry told us that in his forty years of being a businessman, he had learnt that an organisation's efficiency often depended on how its top people were able to predict and influence the changing equations in the playground. And not all the games played in the playground were fair, so one had to be extremely cautious. At times, survival itself was equal to victory.

"People often think that because they are intelligent and smart they will be able to make it to the top. I wish it were so, but the reality is far from it. To survive in the

Playground you need the ability to 'cultivate allies and influence decisions'. Only intelligence and being smart doesn't work here. Even your networking skills are put to the test.

"One of our clients, Mr. Moreno, an importer, used to run a big business in Cuba. However, a few decades ago, the Cuban political scenario changed dramatically. Fidel Castro and his supporters were gaining power in mainstream politics. Some businessmen sensed that if the communists came to power, they would take over the private establishments. So, they secretly started transferring their funds and operations to European countries. However, Mr. Moreno was so keen on ensuring that his internal operations ran smoothly that he ignored the external developments. Then, the inevitable happened. Castro occupied power and commanded that all private property belonging to individuals be taken over by the government. Within no time, Mr. Moreno was stripped of all his assets and reduced to a pauper. His friends had been alert and smart enough to understand what was happening on the Playground and acted accordingly, but Mr. Moreno had to pay a heavy price for his ignorance.

"Take the case of Tata Motors and its Nano project. With assurance of support from the local authorities, they invested huge amounts on a manufacturing plant in West Bengal. The project was to make the world's cheapest car. But as soon as work began, the politicians started troubling them. After weeks of negotiations, the Tatas finally gave up and shifted their project to another state. This forced decision cost them many crores of rupees.

"This is how the Playground works!" Harry said. "For their personal gains, the Politicians, the Press, the Power Brokers, and all the other players adopt a 'use and throw' policy. There are no permanent friends and enemies in the Playground. Depending on the situation, relationships change. And you may be innocent, even Mr. Moreno was innocent, but you will be made a victim for no reason whatsoever.

"So what should one do?" Sam asked.

"Avoid a head-on clash with anybody, but never presume your immunity," Harry suggested, "track the external political and business environment very carefully. Make as many friends as possible, but do not take sides. Maintain neutrality.

"Did I tell you how Dhirubhai Ambani brought the operations of the Bombay Stock Exchange to a stop, for three days?"

"No!" we replied.

"In March 1982, a group of Ambani's rivals decided to put an end to Dhirubhai's business aspirations. But, before I tell you what happened, we need to understand the stock market in those days. In the early 1980s, there were very few traders in the stock market. A daily volume of 50,000 shares was above average. Prices used to fluctuate by a few rupees plus or minus, giving some scope for speculation. And shares were physically sold. On March 18, 1982," Harry said, after checking his diary, "the rival syndicate offloaded 3,50,000 shares of Reliance and its price tumbled from Rs. 131 to Rs. 121 in a few minutes. The selling hysteria shocked the BSE as it witnessed the biggest ever tumble in the Reliance script.

"In was an act of short-selling, where the seller first sells shares he does not own, under the presumption that prices will fall and then purchases the shares at a lower price. The syndicate sold 1.1 million Reliance shares worth over Rs 160 million. The plan was to buy the shares at a cheaper price later. But the plan would only succeed if there was no big buyer who was buying the shares. Reliance was a known name, but no one presumed that its promoter, Dhirubhai, would have the ability to counter such a massive conspiracy.

"Dhirubhai was a keen observer of the Playground and knew quite well that the syndicate did not own the shares and was merely short-selling. Technically, he couldn't buy his own shares as the Indian law did not permit this, so his friends stepped in and purchased about 80 percent of the syndicate's 1.1 million shares.

"In those days every alternate Friday was 'settlement day' when sellers physically delivered the shares to the buyers. On April 30, a Friday, Dhirubhai's friends demanded delivery of the shares that they had purchased from the syndicate. The syndicate displayed its inability to deliver it, and asked for some time. Dhirubhai's brokers agreed, provided they were paid a compensation charge of Rs. 50 for the delay.

"Amidst all this pandemonium, the Bombay Stock Exchange had to be shut for three days. The sellers tried to negotiate a better deal, but Ambani wouldn't budge. He wanted to teach a tough lesson to his rivals. In the days that followed, the price of the Reliance shares soared as the rivals ran helter-skelter to collect every available share. Thankfully for them they were able to honour the delivery and the crisis was sorted out, but it made Dhirubhai Ambani a legend.

"Whenever I meet management students," Harry continued, "I always tell them, efficiency is not determined by buying the best people and technology alone, one has to also track the Playground. Traditionally, like Mr. Moreno, we are so obsessed with our internal environment that we completely ignore the outside world. Had Dhirubhai not been alert about what his rivals were up to, or had his nexus failed in mobilising funds, God knows what would have happened to Reliance."

"What a theory!" Abhi gasped as he took one final look at all the diagrams he had designed. "P for Perfect!"

"And so with this we finally end our discussion on

efficiency and also the GATE model!" Harry said, taking a seat.

All of us also heaved a sigh of relief. It had been four days of intense training.

Then he began to summarise all that we had learnt. "Gigantism, Aggression, Trust, and Efficiency, are the four pillars on which billion dollar organisations are created. If any of them is missing, you will have lopsided growth.

"One of the biggest challenges that multinational companies face is tackling cultural differences. Although it is a difficult obstacle to overcome, my experience proves that when people around the world work around a standardised model it brings tremendous congruency in the organisation. And multinational companies require that. Ever since we have adopted the GATE model in all our offices, I have seen that whether my people are in Manhattan, Manchester, or Mumbai, there is a sense of underlying unity in their way of working."

Harry went on to tell us that it made no sense to work with people who were not aligned to a common vision. He said, "There could be differences of opinion, or differences in ideas, but the vision had to be congruent. And vision wasn't something that was written only in the corner of a corporate office, it is something that guides and fuels your whole organisation.

"Why do you think we spend so much time and money in

these training sessions?" he asked. "Well, the intention is to make you a strong link before linking you to any other part of the chain, because we all know that the chain is as strong as its weakest link. One ineffective person can bring the whole team down. And we don't want people in our company to be weak links."

Harry's words about teamwork reminded me of something I had heard while watching the English Premier League. A coach of a leading club had said, *'No team can win if the players have different agendas'*. Perhaps what Harry was trying to do was to streamline our thinking into a single pattern.

"Tomorrow, I will create a financial blueprint in your mind. This will help you attract lots of money in your life!" his eyes twinkled. "But let's end today's session with one of my favourite examples. It shows how by sharing a common vision we can help each other benefit.

"You must have seen geese flying in the air. Can anyone tell me how they fly?"

"By using their wings," someone said immediately.

Everyone laughed and Harry joined in as well.

"That was a good one. Anyway, back to my question. How do geese fly?"

"They fly in a V-formation," Abhi answered.

"Absolutely correct. But do you know why they fly like that?"

Abhi shook his head, so did everyone else.

"There are many reasons for that. I will take them one by one. First, it is observed that as a bird flaps its wings, it creates an uplift for the bird that follows it. By flying in the shape of a 'V', they add up to 70 percent extra flying range than if each bird flew on its own. Similarly, team members who share a common direction reach their destination quickly and easily, because they are travelling with mutual trust, and lift each other up along the way.

"Second," Harry said, while a photo of geese flying appeared on the screen, "the geese honk to encourage those in front of it, to maintain their speed. This teaches us that words of support energise the whole team. We must always ensure that our honking is encouraging.

"Third, whenever a goose falls out of formation, it automatically feels the drag and resistance of flying alone and quickly gets back into the formation to take advantage of the power of the flock. If we too develop this sense, we will stay aligned to the team's purpose, rather than insisting on sticking to our own personal beliefs.

"And finally, when a goose gets sick or injured, two geese fall out of formation and follow the injured one down to assist it. They stay with him until he is either able to fly, or until he is dead, and then they fly with another formation to catch up with their group. This noble gesture teaches us to stand beside each other when times get rough.

"Remember," Harry said, "With effective teamwork, common people can achieve uncommon results."

An efficient team is one that beats with one heart.

———

IF YOU WAIT FOR ALL THE LIGHTS TO TURN GREEN, YOU WILL NEVER GET STARTED ON YOUR TRIP TO THE TOP

—ZIG ZIGLAR

That evening we received an SMS from Harry.

'I have forwarded an email to you. Please check it.'

"From where did he get our numbers?" I asked Abhi.

"Saloni must have it," he said as he switched on his laptop to read the mail.

After a minute or so, he jumped up with joy, "Boy, you got to see this! It's very inspiring!"

I turned the screen towards me and started reading the mail.

Dear Abhi and Dave,

We have always used the word 'because' for excuses and to reduce our efficiency.

But the word 'because' is made up of two words — 'be' and 'cause'.

'Be' refers to being involved and 'cause' refers to good work.

So, do not use the word because to give excuses. Instead, use it to empower yourself.

BE A CAUSE in creating change.

BE A CAUSE in keeping people happy.

BE A CAUSE in making this world a better place!

You must have heard of an oyster. It is a small mollusc that lives in the sea. Occasionally, a grain of sand enters the oyster's shell and starts irritating the sensitive tissue. But, instead of complaining that 'the sea didn't take enough care of me' or 'because the shell was not properly closed', the oyster takes responsibility of things. With full efficiency it single-mindedly engages in the task of getting rid of the grain of sand.

And guess what happens in the process?

By 'becoming a cause', the oyster transforms a useless, common grain of sand into a priceless, rare pearl!

As humans we can learn a great lesson from this. Whenever life throws us an obstacle, instead of complaining 'because of this, because of that' we can simply choose to 'be (a) cause' and convert that same adversity into an opportunity to create something better!

CREATING A BLUEPRINT

"Before I start today's session, I want to ask all of you a question. If your answer is 'yes' then raise your hand, and if your answer is 'no' you will not raise your hand. Is that all right?" Harry asked.

"Yes," we all responded.

"Alright then. I want to know how many of you are currently facing a financial problem?"

Nobody raised their hand.

"It could be anything," Harry continued, "having a huge loan on your head; being unable to buy your dream home; or a car; accumulated business losses; undervalued stocks; inadequate income to fulfil your needs, just anything."

People started looking around at each other. I wanted to raise my hand, but felt reluctant. How could I disclose my personal financial problems to a group of strangers?

"Now don't let your ego stand in the way," he said, sensing our discomfort. "If you have a problem, just raise your hand. Why are you shy? Did I not admit that I too had been through a lean phase in my life?"

I looked at Abhi. He was looking puzzled too.

"Saloni," Harry called out to his PA. "It seems that everybody out here is financially sound. So there is no need to teach them the 'Three Secret Laws of Money'. Let's call it a day."

Harry closed the red diary and removed his glasses. "You guys can go back to your dorms," he said and started walking away.

"Nooo!" some people in the last row screamed.

"Yesss!" he replied. "If none of you has the disease, what's the use of giving you the medicine?"

"I need it," one lady raised her hand boldly.

After her, a few others also raised their hands. Within a minute, almost 80 percent of the participants, including me and Abhi, had raised our hands. What surprised me was that even some senior executives, who supposedly had good pay packages, had also raised their hands.

There was silence in the room, everyone was waiting for Harry to speak.

"Aha! That's nice," Harry stopped walking. He wore his glasses again, and looked at all of us. "It takes some guts to publicly accept you have a financial problem."

He made a gesture at Saloni who was still sitting and smiling. Perhaps she was aware that Harry hadn't really planned to cancel the session, and had just played a mind game with us.

"It happens in every lecture," Harry said, smiling wryly. "Initially, everybody hesitates to acknowledge the problem, but then 80-90 percent of participants admit that they have a financial problem. But, I always play this game, because I want you to be upfront about whatever problem you are facing. Otherwise you will only be behaving like an ostrich. Do you know what the 'ostrich mentality' refers to?

"No," we said.

"Alright, I will tell you. When an ostrich is attacked, it digs a hole in the ground with its legs and then closes its eyes, and buries its head in the hole. The ostrich presumes that since it cannot see its enemy, even the enemy cannot see it. And guess what, because of its ignorance it falls prey.

"The science of Ontology says that we, too, try to run away from problems that creep into our lives and then we presume that since we are distant from our problems, they too are distant from us. But the truth is that 'whatever you resist, will persist'. So the best approach is to accept what is in front of us, and then create a strategy to combat it, because *change begins only when you accept reality.*

Harry switched on the screen, and a slide with three circles appeared.

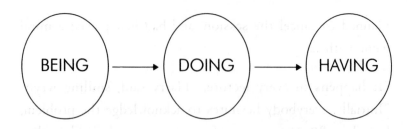

"Take a look at the screen. We have already studied 'Being' and 'Doing.' Now comes the last and final part 'Having'."

"'Having' is a very critical phenomenon, because that is the ultimate aim of all our actions. We are all concerned with 'having an outcome', or 'obtaining a result.' In fact, each of our actions is motivated by the final outcome. It is the desire to 'have' something which motivates us to act in the first place.

"Unfortunately, money is one area which remains unresolved in most people's lives. However hard they try, money seems to elude them. I have seen people who are 'Doing' all sorts of work, yet are only able to 'Have' very little money. And this lack of money causes further tension, stress, health issues, strains in relationships, and often gives rise to an inferiority complex."

Harry told us that Om Group had a clear mission statement. The highest priority was given to 'profit maximisation and wealth creation'. And as part of the Group, our task was to create wealth — for the company, for our investors, for our stakeholders, and for ourselves.

"But people have a very anti-money mentality," he pointed

out. "Forget about creating wealth, they don't even like to discuss it. Ever since they are born they are conditioned with statements like, 'money is evil'; 'money is bad'; 'money is the root cause of all misery'; etc.

"People even go to the extent of saying that 'money is un-spiritual' and having too much money will create all sorts of problems in your life.

"Because of such conditioning, one lives with an anti-money mentality. The fact of the Universe is that *'outlook becomes outcome'*. So, if your outlook towards money is negative, then there is nothing surprising about the fact that the outcome in your life will also be negative."

Harry told us to think about a blueprint. He told us that every architect first designs a blueprint of the desired structure, and based on it the actual building is created. The building is nothing but a manifestation of the blueprint. If the blueprint is perfect, the building is perfect, but if the blueprint is improper, the building will be improper. Each one of us too has a financial blueprint in our mind. If the financial blueprint is perfect, money will flow smoothly into our lives. But, if the financial blueprint is in a mess, our relationship with money will also be in a mess.

"The fact that a person has financial problems suggests that something is wrong with his blueprint. His beliefs and notions about money are improper and that is why it is not flowing in easily. So, unless I clear that mess first, unless I erase the wrong blueprint, I cannot replace it with a new and perfect model."

He walked to one corner of the stage and showed us a glass of water.

"Presume that the water in this glass is muddy. Now, if I want to fill this glass with pure water I cannot do so by simply pouring in pure water. I will first have to empty the muddy water, only then can I refill it. Similarly, any new ideology or belief system cannot be imprinted unless the existing belief system is done away with.

"Today, I will eliminate all the negative notions about money that have been implanted in your brain by society. We will erase the faulty blueprint so we can create a new one in its place.

"The journey is going to be exciting, shocking, and cathartic, Harry smiled mysteriously. "But I urge you to have an open mind and most importantly, be receptive to what I say."

A new slide appeared on screen.

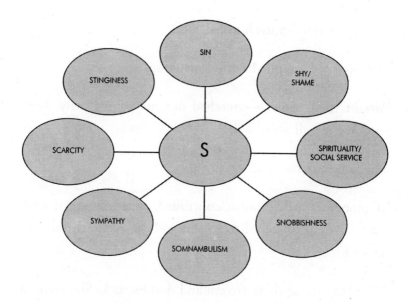

"You can see that many words are written around the letter 'S'. I have purposely used words beginning with a common letter so you can remember it easily. But I want you to remember them only for the sake of forgetting; for each of these words are actually 'notions' or 'attitudes' towards wealth which obstruct the flow of money in your life.

"Moving clockwise, the first word is 'Sin'. It is one of the most common feelings why people resent wealth. Right since childhood we are told that money is a very bad thing and earning money is a sin.

"My friend, Suresh Padmanabhan, was conducting a workshop on money. He told the participants that money is a wonderful thing and one must enjoy it. After the session, an old lady walked up to him and said, 'How can you say money is wonderful? Don't you know it is evil?'

'Money is evil?' Suresh asked her.

'Yes, it is,' she replied with conviction.

'Alright then,' Suresh stretched out his palms, 'why don't you give me all your evil?'

The lady was taken aback.

'If money is evil,' Suresh continued, 'why carry evil with you? Give me all of what you have. I am ready to take it,' he said.

"The lady stood there frozen and dumbstruck. She realised it was not possible for her to part with her wealth, howsoever evil she might think it was.

"'I have met many such people who criticise money,' Suresh told me later, 'most of them believe it is against religion to earn it. But, my simple question to them is that if it is unholy, then why do priests keep cash boxes inside places of worship. Ask them to stop this practice, and they will shun the idea!'"

"Excuse me, sir," a participant interrupted, "then why do all gurus condemn money?"

"It is nothing but hypocrisy," Harry replied. "They condemn it so that you don't hold it for too long, and give it to them."

"But the guru doesn't even touch the donations."

"Yes, he does not. But his obedient disciples readily do it for him. So it is one and the same thing, isn't it? The guru advises people to lead a simple life, but his own lifestyle is usually one of luxury."

The participant seemed only partly convinced, there was still some doubt in his mind. Harry sensed this and removed a penknife from his pocket.

"What is this?" he asked the participant.

"A knife."

"Good, now tell me, is it a good thing or a bad thing?"

"A bad thing."

"Why?" Harry asked, he looked sad.

"Because you can stab someone with it."

"And what if I use it in the kitchen to cut vegetables?"

"Then it is a good thing."

"So, ultimately, is it a good thing or a bad thing?"

"It is neither good, nor bad. It is just neutral. It depends on how you use it."

"And what about this?" Harry removed a hundred-rupee note from his wallet and waved it. "Is this good or bad?"

"This is also neutral," the participant seemed to have got the insight. "It depends on how you use it."

"Yes, you can use it for a good cause, or use it for something bad, depending on your intent, but by itself it is just a neutral tool. And can there be anything sinful about possessing a neutral tool?"

"No sir!"

Harry reminded us that earlier the barter system prevailed in our society. But it was too difficult to practice since mutual needs were often difficult to satisfy. If one wanted a book and only had a shirt to barter, then he had to look out for someone who would be willing to take the shirt and offer the book. These mutual exchanges created unnecessary complications, and therefore money was invented as a simple substitute.

"Unfortunately, the invention that was supposed to simplify our lives," he still carried the note in his hand, "has created the greatest emotional burden. Ranging from hatred to greed and the desire to 'show-off' we have assigned all possible emotions to this neutral tool, which perhaps explains why there are so many complications surrounding money. We will soon install a new, positive blueprint in your minds, but for the time being I urge you to just think of money as a neutral tool. Keep all thoughts of sin aside."

"Next, we move to another dangerous set of emotions

associated with money, namely, 'Shy' and 'Shame'.

"I will tell you about an incident that really happened. Many years ago, we were interviewing a candidate for a post in Om Group. The interview panel consisted of two HR executives and myself. The boy was intelligent and answered most of our questions correctly, but when I asked him what his expected salary was, he suddenly felt uneasy.

'What package you are expecting from the company?' I asked.

'Well...er...money is not a big concern, sir,' he tried to deflect the question.

'But you would have some figure in your mind.'

'Not really sir. Whatever you give me is fine.'

"When I tried to grill him further, his discomfort with money started becoming apparent. Had it not been for this, the last set of answers, I would have selected him," Harry confessed. "But I did not. When my HR guys asked me why, I told them *A person who does not know his own value, can never make our company valuable!*"

The auditorium erupted in applause. "Superb!" Abhi nodded his head in approval.

"It is not that candidate alone, I have met so many people who are ready to discuss everything, but when money comes up, they feel extremely shy and ashamed to ask for it. They will divert the question by giving cliché reasons like, 'money ain't a big thing'; 'whatever you give me is fine'; 'let's get started on the work, money we will see later'.

"Some people are so ashamed about asking for money that they would rather do your work for free just to 'look good' in your eyes. Personally speaking, I would prefer to earn what I rightfully deserve and see some green stuff in my wallet rather than have an empty wallet just to look good for someone else. And it is one of my deepest beliefs that if you continue doing stuff for free, or at a lower price, people will not only discount your value but will also take you for granted."

"But, being upfront about money makes you look like a selfish person," a girl objected.

"It is not selfishness, dear, it is self-concern," Harry corrected her. "We are all concerned about ourselves and there is nothing wrong with that. And moreover, when I say you must be upfront and straightforward about money, it does not only mean being clear about your receipts, but also being clear about your payments."

"Meaning?" she asked.

"You must be equally eager to pay people. Like for example, when we designed Om Group's first website, Sameer was still in engineering college. He was extremely excited about technology and so I shared the project details with him. But, he didn't approve of the idea of paying money to a professional web designer since one of his senior friends in college could do it for us for free.

'Your friend will do it for free, but that will cost you more,' I warned.

'How come?' he asked.

'Two reasons. First, since he is doing it free, he will work as per his own whims and fantasies. I can't compel him to work under a deadline like the way I would do with a professional. When you are at people's mercy, you can't dictate your terms.'

'And the second reason?' he asked.

'The second is more dangerous. If he is doing it for free, he is placing an obligation on you. Tomorrow, he may ask you to do something for him, which you don't want to, but you will be under tremendous emotional pressure to oblige. It is better to pay money and close the matter.'

"He thought for a minute and said, 'Yes dad, I think you're correct.'"

Harry looked at the girl and summarised, "If you are only being upfront with your receipts, people will consider you selfish. But, if you are equally upfront about your payments, then they will consider you to be 'fair'."

"Yes, now it is clear," she said.

"I am not asking you to be a 'money-minded' individual," Harry clarified. "If you genuinely want to do something for free, you can. But that's a different thing. Here I am talking about those transactions where you want to 'ask' but are feeling 'shy' and 'ashamed'."

Personally this session was turning out to be extremely insightful for me. One of my problems was that I could never tell 'no' to anybody. Many of my friends had taken small loans from me and had not returned my money. Often I tried to muster up some courage and ask for the money, but the thought of losing a friend held me back. Some loans were long overdue, but they just didn't bother. It was then that Harry's words gave me an insight into what my problem really was. He said that if people do not experience any shame in taking things from you, why should you feel ashamed in asking for it? Also, one who is not considerate about you, isn't worthy to be your friend in the first place. So why bother about such people?

"The Banias always insist on separating their professional life from their personal life," Harry said. "They say, 'relatives are most welcome to have dinner with us at home, but in offices that must pay what they owe us'."

He then brought our attention to the next few words on the screen — 'Spirituality/Social Service'.

"This is one of my favourite discussions," Harry suddenly brightened. "All my life I have fought for it!"

"As businessmen we are constantly criticised for being 'unconcerned about social service and public welfare'. A leading exporter was once accused by a journalist of not doing any social service.

"But he was quick to reply, 'You mean to say I am not doing any social service? We provide employment to thousands of people who nurture thousands of families. Countless distributors, retailers and traders have got business opportunities because of us. Then there are half a million shareholders who have purchased their dream homes, dream cars, educated their children, and visited foreign countries because of the money they invested in our shares. Is this not social service? Are they not part of society?

'But sir, I was talking about the type of work NGOs do — going to orphanages, visiting old age homes,' the journalist clarified.

'This is also a type of social service. I am not denying it. What we are doing is also social service. Every year we pay millions to the government as taxes, which helps them build infrastructure, provide education, and take care of the environment. But in spite of this people still think businessmen do not serve society. How disgusting! Business is the greatest form of social service. It is businesses that help create wealth, meet demands with supply and create employment. Had it not been for the funds provided by business people there would not be a single charitable institution in the world.'

"The journalist was speechless. But the exporter continued, 'Charity, no doubt, is a very good means of social service, but it is only a temporary solution. You may occasionally give someone a plate of food, or a pair of clothes, but business houses generate long-term employment which helps people pay for their own food and clothing, without relying on someone else's mercy.'

"Friends," Harry said, "remove this belief that earning money and serving society are two conflicting activities. They are one and the same. You cannot serve society with empty pockets. In fact, in the ancient Vedic scriptures they divided human life in four different phases. For the first 25 years of his life an individual is asked to only focus on gaining knowledge and developing skills that will help him earn money. Then from ages 26-50 he has to fulfil social obligations and focus on creating wealth. He must create cash flows that would last a lifetime for his people. As a youngster, one is physically more capable of earning wealth. Then, from age 51 onwards begins the third phase where an individual is urged to gradually retire from financial activities, pass his business to worthy successors, and engage himself in social service. And after enough social service, begins the last phase where he is supposed to pursue spirituality. This is a time-tested model which the ancient Aryans have followed for over 10,000 years."

"So the emphasis is on first earning money for oneself,

and then serving others, right?" a participant asked.

"Precisely," Harry said. "First, you create your competency to earn, next you earn enough to support yourself, and finally go out and impact society. It is a very rational approach, isn't it? Unfortunately, many youngsters get this whole model wrong. When they are young they spend their time in social and spiritual activities, putting their studies and work aside. Later, when they are old they are forced to work because enough wealth was not created in their youth.

"Right now, I volunteer at Saroon, run this centre, and conduct seminars. But, I do not have to bother about funds. During my youth I worked towards creating my cash flows. Now, I can sit back and relax. My dividend and interest incomes will easily take care of all my expenses and social contributions.

"I hope I have clarified this point," Harry said. "Money helps you serve society and pursue spirituality. Without it, you cannot pursue either.

"We will quickly run through the next two points 'Snobbishness' and 'Somnambulism'.

"There is a proverb in English, 'a little success is a dangerous thing' and quite rightly so, because after the first feel of success and wealth, it often goes to the head and inflates the ego to such an extent that the individual becomes snobbish. He starts behaving with a 'holier than thou' attitude, treating others with disdain. And it is precisely this ego which restricts his ability to grow and earn more.

"Has anyone of you used old Swiss watches?" Harry asked. "I doubt if they are available these days. These watches were made of 17 jewels with a mainspring which required regular winding. It is said that the Swiss watches enjoyed market domination for years until 'Quartz' technology arrived. The quartz watches were thinner, lighter, cheaper, and didn't require winding. But, the Swiss were so obsessed with their success and monopoly that they ignored this technology. Guess what happened. The Japanese captured this opportunity and started making quartz watches. People liked them and switched over to Japanese watches in no time. The Swiss lost their exalted position. This is a perfect example of how success leads to snobbishness, and snobbishness leads to downfall.

"Dhirubhai had once said, 'One thing you will never find in me is an inflated ego. I am willing to salute anyone in the government, be it a top boss, or a door attendant.'

"It was this attitude which always kept him on a roll," Harry said. "If you had an idea, he was all ears, no matter who you were. When he was about to enter his car, he wouldn't wait for the chauffeur to open the door, just because he was a rich man. He would walk around the car and open the door himself, because it saved time. During lunch in the factory he would affectionately put an arm around the shoulder of his labourer and enquire about his health and say, 'Hope everything is good!'

"Dhirubhai's down-to-earth attitude was scoffed at by other arrogant businessmen who didn't feel it necessary to mingle with the common man in a factory. But Dhirubhai perhaps knew better. It was his 'friendly' approach that helped him earn people's loyalty and trust.

Harry's message was clear. One must keep his self-righteous, snobbish attitude aside. Ideas often come from the most unexpected quarters and no one should be underestimated. Bill Gates was once asked, who is Microsoft's biggest competitior? In reply, Gates did not mention Google, or Apple, or IBM. He said that he was afraid of 15-16 year old kids with their fresh, young minds, and revolutionary ideas. Just one great idea, effectively executed, and it could pose a threat to Microsoft!

"Once, it so happened that a toothpaste manufacturing company had called a meeting of its top executives. The agenda was to increase sales. The seniors were brainstorming, when a young, not-so-important executive put forth his idea. He suggested that the mouth of the toothpaste tube be widened. Some egoistic seniors scoffed at such a dumb idea. But one senior executive realised that it was a brilliant suggestion. Every time someone would press the tube, more paste would come out, which would exhaust the tube faster compelling a quicker repurchase.

"Usually, when we talk about increasing sales we tend to focus on market strategy and advertising. But at times a seemingly trivial suggestion can produce miracles!

"Next we come to 'Somnambulism'," Harry moved on.

"'Somnambulism' is a medical term to describe people who have the tendency of doing things when they are asleep, but here I am using it to describe people who have a tendency of sleeping when they are doing things. In other words, I am referring to those people who lead their lives without any aim, planning, or enthusiasm; dragging along, and living life just for the heck of it.

"Youngsters, at the peak of their careers, are absolutely blank about what they want in life. They waste days and months doing the most unproductive things, never really taking charge of their lives. I too had 'fallen out of track' in my youth and succumbed to addictions and it took me a long time to come back on track," Harry confessed.

"Somnambulists are able to create wealth but experience difficulty in sustaining it. Their unconscious spending erodes all their wealth leaving them with a paltry residue.

"Just recently I read in the newspapers that Daryll Strawberry, the famous baseball player was such a 'spend-a-holic' who never saved money. Strawberry churned a fortune by playing baseball, something like $3-5 million a year. Add to it the millions he must have made through celebrity endorsements, brand rights, autograph signings, and public appearances. Let us say he made something between $75-100 million during his career. Yet, by the age of 40 he was broke! His expensive lifestyle, cars, houses, drugs, and alcohol rehabilitation bills eroded all his savings. His wife complained to the media that Daryll wasn't even able to pay the maintenance money that he owed to his children."

We were told that self-discipline was the primary virtue that one needs to cultivate while handling money. Harry was not against a luxurious lifestyle, because he himself led one. Harry owned a Rolls Royce and had a palatial bungalow in one of the richest areas in Mumbai. But he had spent the money 'consciously' being fully aware of his financial position.

"Make a resolution to yourself, no matter whatever the circumstances, every month you will save and invest a minimum of ten percent of your earnings. Even if you owe a debt to someone, keep aside ten percent of what you earn, and pay from the remaining amount.

Harry suggested that saving for five years in the early part of our career would almost double the amount in our bank by the time we retired. Abhi confirmed this.

"So, I hope I have made myself clear. I am not against spending or leading a comfortable life. I am only against 'unconscious wasting' which if unchecked can become a fatally destructive habit."

Harry took a breather. It had been a long session. He seemed to be a little tired today.

"We have covered five points," he looked at the slide. "Three more points — 'Sympathy', 'Scarcity', and 'Stinginess' are left. However, today we will discuss only 'Sympathy' as the other two points require understanding the 'First Secret Law of Money' which we will discuss tomorrow.

"'Sympathy'," he scribbled on the whiteboard, "is the most dangerous of all the elements in the circle. This seemingly innocent virtue will help protect your ego but will destroy your career.

"During a conference in Bengaluru, I met a man who told me something strange. He said that the government had given free flats to a few slumdwellers in his vicinity. Initially, the man was happy because he thought the slum dwellers would get a chance to live a better life. But, he was surprised to find that in a few weeks most slumdwellers had rented out the free flat and had started living in a slum in another part of the city. And the money that was earned through rent was spent on alcohol and gambling!

"Even Prof. Malthus, a renowned economist, reached a similar conclusion. He spent many years studying the lives of the downtrodden and concluded that if you give money to poor people, their life does not become better. Instead, they continue to have more children as long as they are able to maintain a basic rate of survival.

"Such realities are often disturbing," Harry said, "especially for someone like me who has now devoted his whole life to serving humanity. But, I was keen to understand why people cling to misery and so I started my research on the subject. After going through many books on Ontology, I came across a very relevant statement — People love to live in misery because it gives meaning to their life. If you take away their misery, their life becomes very hollow. Then they lose the entertainment that they had by complaining and cribbing through the day.

"Sympathy acts like a massage to injured egos," Harry continued, "and some people get some kind of pleasure by seeking it.

"When I came to Saroon, many people told me that the 'lack of knowledge of English' acts as a major obstruction to their careers, and had they known English, they would have really made it big in life.

"With a desire to help them, we brought in the best English language trainers from Mumbai and started offering classes to the locals. For the first few days, the venue was packed, but as time went by, attendance declined. After a few days, 70 percent students had dropped out, but the remaining students showed some eagerness to continue. I asked my HR personnel to find out why people were not attending the classes. They spoke to the participants but were disappointed with their silly excuses. One participant who was attending classes regularly gave them a very candid reply. He said, 'Most people out here will never make a genuine attempt to learn English.'

'And why would that be?' the HR officer asked.

'Because not knowing English is generally accepted as a valid reason for all sorts of failures. And if people learn the language, how can they use it as an excuse to defend their failures?'

'And what would that achieve?'

'Well, without the excuse their incompetence would be exposed, which will hurt their ego. So they prefer hiding behind the 'but I don't know English' excuse rather than be answerable to people's expectations.'

"I was shattered when I heard this! What the boy was saying was 100 percent right," Harry said.

"Human beings are highly egoistic. Whenever they fail, they don't want to take responsibility of their own actions, they seek an external excuse to justify their failure.

"They say things like, 'because of this I couldn't do it', 'because of that I wasn't able to succeed'...And once they get a valid excuse, they stick to it like glue because it helps us shield our ego and justify our failures.

"Folks, tell me honestly, how many times do you and I also behave like this? We not only invent excuses and reasons, but also cling to them as self-defence. You agree with me?"

"Yes," we all agreed.

"In these parts of the world, it is not rare to find such people. At the age of 20, people will complain that they don't know English. Ten years later, they will still complain that they don't know English. Thirty more years later, at the age of 60, they will still say that they don't know English. An entire lifetime will be spent clinging to an excuse but they will not invest a few months of their life and a few thousand rupees to learn a language that will boost their careers, and increase their income.

"Barbara Pais, a participant in one of my earlier seminars had a similar story. After her internship as an accounts assistant, she was jobless for a substantial period of time. But she didn't want to take the blame on herself. It was too embarrassing. So she started thinking of all possible excuses. Basically, a good excuse was the one which would — take the blame away from her; appear valid; and be easily accepted by people.

"Her mind started conjuring up all kinds of a perfect excuse. Finally, she found the perfect one. She started telling people 'It's all because of the recession'. Whenever someone would ask her about her work, she would conveniently transfer the blame to the 'recession'. And people would give her that 'oh, what a poor girl' look and try to cheer her up. This sympathy was very comforting, and she started enjoying the game. For months she was jobless, sitting at home and telling people that it was because of the recession. Perchance during that same period, Barbara attended this seminar and realised that what she was doing was nothing but 'melodrama'. Clinging to excuses would shield her ego, but would not solve the problem. It was a powerful realisation. From the very next day she started focusing on her core strengths and how she could capitalise on it. I did a powerful technique with her called 'Dream Manifestation' which I will do with you one of these days," Harry said.

"So, coming back to the subject, Barbara realised that she had a strong inclination towards creativity. Often she would spend hours in front of the computer making designs. But it made more sense reaching out to companies, rather than just work for herself. Since she didn't have any clients, she would do the work for free, looking for a break. Every morning, she would read the newspaper and look for advertisements that were not well designed. Then, she would work on her computer, re-design the ad and email it to the company with her professional details. If she went to a restaurant, she would take the menu card, redesign the aesthetic elements, and give it back to the owner. One such client for whom she did a print ad was so impressed with her work that he called her up and hired her services for his print ad campaign. Barbara seized the opportunity and went ahead. She did not only design the print campaign, but also gave him a complimentary redesign of his corporate brochure and pamphlets. The overwhelmed client thanked Barbara and referred her name to his colleagues as well. It's just been two months, but you won't believe it, Barbara now has two people working with her, and is planning to start her own design firm.

"Remember," he said, *"When man makes a determined decision, he suddenly achieves a power greater than the combined might of all his surrounding circumstances!* Then all excuses of the 'recession', 'I don't know English', 'only if I had more money', 'only if I had more time', 'only if I had better education', 'only if I were born in another country', 'only if luck supported me', 'only if I had a different coloured skin', all these lose significance. Seeking sympathy acts as an obstacle to the flow of wealth. It may shield your ego but will not fill your pockets."

Harry had one final look at the circular diagram and switched off the projector.

"So with this we complete all the elements that block money from flowing in your life. From tomorrow onwards, for the next three days, I will teach you the three secret laws of money. I must say you guys are really lucky, because we have never discussed these laws in any of our seminars before. But since this is my last public talk, I want to ensure that this wisdom reaches the whole world.

"But, before I end today's session I would like to confess something. In my seminars, I often meet participants like Barbara who are going through testing times in their life. Some people are unemployed, some people are underpaid, some are still working hard to get a break in their career. Despite their best attempts they have only faced rejection. Under such circumstances, it is but natural, that one starts doubting his or her self-worth and feels that one does not deserve the great riches and wealth life has to offer. So this one goes out to all such people seated here."

Harry removed his wallet.

"Take a look at this," he took out a crisp new Rs. 1000 note. "How many of you want this?"

Everybody raised their hands enthusiastically.

"Good. Now suppose I were to fold this note and offer it to you. Would you still want it?"

"Yes," we roared.

"Excellent. Now suppose I were to crush this note in my palm and then offer it to you, would you still want it?"

"Yes!"

"Yes, why not!"

"Of course!" said everyone.

"Now, I am not going to do it, but suppose if I were to place this note on the floor and stamp on it with my shoe, would you still want it?"

"Yeesss!" we replied, feeling a little irritated now.

"Why?" he asked suddenly, with a stern expression on his face.

"Because whether you fold it, or crush it or stamp on it, the value of the note is still the same," a participant answered.

"Superb!" Harry's eyes glittered. "That is exactly the point I want to convey. Please remember that each one of us is valuable, like this Rs. 1000 note.

"At times, life can be really tough with us. It may squeeze us dry, crush us, or throw extremely tough times at us. But whatever life deals us," he raised the note above his head and said, "our value remains the same!"

"Never, ever, ever discount your self-worth."

———

That night I didn't sleep well. What Harry had told us was so exciting that it kept me awake till late at night. In the next three days, he was going to teach us the 'Three Secret Laws of Money'! These were extraordinary principles directly inspired by nature, which always worked with unfaltering accuracy and precision.

"Although I will be using money as a standard example," Harry had clarified, "you need not restrict yourself to money. You can use the same laws to create whatever you want in life, be it health, relationships, career, happiness…. virtually anything that you want."

He had also said that once you start understanding and applying these laws, there is nothing in the world that you cannot achieve!

Now, you tell me, when such celestial knowledge is about to be revealed, how could one sleep?

THE FIRST SECRET LAW
OF MONEY

"There is a lady by the name of Rhonda Byrne," Harry began. "Not too long ago, she had undertaken a research project on the minds of some of the world's greatest people, including big names like Albert Einstein, Beethoven, Emerson, Lincoln, Edison, and many others. The surprising thing that Byrne discovered was that there was something common among all these people. All of them understood what is called the 'Law of Attraction'. It was precisely their understanding of this law that made them rich, famous, and successful.

"Today we shall discuss this law of attraction which will lead us to the 'First Secret Law of Money'.

Harry walked towards a table and threw a pen. And then turning towards us, asked, "Why did the pen fall down?"

"Because of gravity," we replied.

"Correct. Now consider this. There is a tribe in Africa, where the people have no knowledge of Newton's Law of Gravity. There, if the tribal chief throws a pen, will it still fall down?"

"Yes."

"The point I am trying to make is simple — whether you have knowledge about gravity or not, it will still work on you. Whether you believe in it or not, the law will still hold good.

"When I discuss the 'Three Secret Laws', some people do not believe in what I say. But I always tell them, whether you believe in it or not, the laws will still work on you."

Harry showed us a picture of a huge transmission tower, very similar to the ones installed by mobile operators.

"The First Secret Law is called the 'Law of Attraction'. It says that everything that comes into our lives has been attracted by us. And it is attracted by three different signals that we send to the Universe. First, are the images that we hold in our minds. Second, the statements that we assert to ourselves and others, and third, the emotions and feelings that we hold in our body.

"So, thoughts, words, and feelings," he counted off his fingers and pointed right back at the tower.

"Consider your mind to be like this transmission tower. All these signals are being continuously transmitted by your mind to the Universe, and the Universe replies by giving you objects, events, and circumstances that match your signals."

"So you mean that my thoughts actually attract whatever I get in my life?" someone asked.

"Yes. To put in simple words, the law of attraction says that, *'thoughts become things'*, or *'outlook becomes outcome'*. Just yesterday I told you about the architect who first creates a blueprint of a building and then the actual building is constructed using the blueprint as a guide. Quite similarly, you too are the architect of your life. The thoughts, feelings, emotions, and beliefs that you generate create a blueprint in your mind and based on this blueprint the Universe creates your actual life. It is said that whatever takes place in our world, takes place twice — first in your mind and then in the outside world. So, it is very critical to have the perfect blueprint, because just as a positive blueprint will give you positive results, a negative blueprint will give you negative results."

Harry told us that the Universe is like a genie that we have seen in movies. And like Aladdin's genie, the Universe also fulfils all our desires. But the only difference is that while the genie fulfils his master's desires instantly, the Universe fulfils our desires when it feels it is the best time to do so.

He showed us a picture of the genie obediently bowing down to Aladdin and saying, 'Your wish is my command.'

"If you understand this picture, you will understand the 'First Secret Law of Money'."

There was sudden silence in the hall. People were on the edge of their seats. I stopped writing and was all ears.

Harry walked toward the whiteboard and wrote,

MONEY IS A MANIFESTATION
OF YOUR MENTALITY

"Yes, my dear friends, this is the first secret law — Money is the manifestation of your mentality.

"All the wealth that we have ever achieved, or failed to achieve, is because we had a certain attitude towards money, and the Universe manifested it. In Physics they say, 'Like attracts like', the same law can be applied here, but we are actually talking at the level of thought.

"So if you are a pessimist who grumbles about money all the time, or you are a cynic who is sceptical about your future cash flow, then you are constantly emitting signals of doubt and disbelief to the Universe. Therefore, like an obedient genie, it responds by creating more financial troubles for you.

"On the other hand, if you are positive about money and comfortable with it, you are sending signals of receptivity to the Universe. It then says, 'Your wish is my command, master', and creates more and more wealth for you.

"So, the law of attraction does not care whether you hold positive or negative images in your mind. It will simply give you more of what you are emitting. Perhaps that is why people who are constantly worried about debts end up attracting more debts. If they really want to get out of debt, they must focus on financial freedom and must try to think and feel that freedom, which will then be manifested as per their thoughts."

Harry told us that he had studied the lives of many millionaires who had gone bankrupt due to various reasons, but because their mind was focused on creating wealth they were easily able to bounce back.

"There was a time when Dhirubhai was under terrible financial constraints. The government had cancelled his production licenses and even his stock prices had plummeted. The financial condition took a toll on his health and he suffered a paralytic stroke from which he never fully recovered. Some of you would know that one of Dhirubhai's hands was numb due to paralysis for the last thirty years of his life. But the point I am trying to make is that even during extreme financial and physical problems, Dhirubhai was never worried or concerned about money. Instead, he focused all his energy and attention on just one question, 'How do I get out of here?' Day in and day out, he single-mindedly focused on just that one thought, and the Universe responded by matching all the right events and circumstances which helped him get out of the financial slump."

He gave us examples of rich people who sometimes lost their wealth, but were able to regain it in no time. The Parsees who had to leave Persia were virtually bankrupt when they came to India, but they never considered themselves beggars. In their mind, they were still rich folk and this attitude helped them manifest wealth back into their lives. It was a similar story with the Sindhis who had to leave Pakistan, or the Jews who had to run away from Hitler's reach. All these communities were able to attract wealth into their lives. But, on the other hand, the habitually poor are so confirmed and certain about their poverty, that they end up attracting all natural calamities, diseases, and accidents which erode their savings from time to time.

"We often hear of people who win million dollar lotteries. But we have never heard of these lottery winners using these millions and become multi-millionaires? Why? Because for 30-40 years they have conditioned their minds about being 'middle-class' people who live with an 'average' income. So when they receive a windfall, their mind is not able to sustain it and gets rid of it.

"Friends, the first secret says that 'money is a manifestation of your mentality'. So if your mentality is that of an 'average' man, you will only be able to attract average wealth.

"Some time back there was a television show in USA called *Who wants to be a Millionaire?* Quite a few of the show's participants became millionaires. But, when a private publication surveyed them, it was surprising to note that after a few years all participants were back to Square One. Personally, I was not surprised with the survey findings. Deep in their mind, their financial blueprint was still that of a common man and therefore they were not able to sustain their 'millionaire status' for long.

"So, the first definite action you must take is to accept the fact that you are a rich person. Whether you are actually rich, or not, is immaterial because if the attitude is right, you are going to attract riches."

We were told that the output of anything could be altered by changing the input. To increase the mileage of a car, one had to change the quality of the fuel supplied to it, or to alter the output of a computer program one had to change its codes. Quite similarly, if one wanted to witness positive results in the outer world, one first had to change the beliefs that are held in the mind.

"I have heard that when PepsiCo CEO and chairwoman, Indra Nooyi was a young school girl, her mother used to play a game with her called 'President'. Her mother would give her a new task every day, and Indra's job was to solve it from the point of view of India's President. Her mother would urge her to approach the problem as if she was a top-level leader taking every aspect into consideration. The little girl's mind was systematically cultivated to be that of a 'big boss'. Little wonder then that she ended up becoming CEO of PepsiCo.

"It is also said that when Shivaji, the great Maratha king, was a toddler, his mother would sing songs while addressing him as 'Raja', the Indian word for 'King'. She had instructed everyone in the family to call him Raja, till the boy's mind was absolutely certain about it. That is why he ended up becoming one of the greatest kings the subcontinent has ever had. So you see, it's not only money, but everything that happens in your life that is a manifestation of your mentality."

"Sir, with all due respect to your knowledge, I find it difficult to believe what you are saying. Can you give any solid evidence in support of your claims?" a lady seated in the middle row asked.

"Why not?" Harry said. "Take a look at some of the famous quotes given by great men of our times. They have all testified to what I am saying," new slides appeared on the screen as he said this.

> You create your Universe as you go along.
> —Winston Churchill
>
> Imagination is everything. It is the preview of life's coming attractions.
> —Albert Einstein
>
> Whatever the mind can conceive, it can achieve.
> —W. Clement Stone
>
> When it comes to creating wealth, it is a mindset. It's all about how you think.
> —David Schirmer
>
> Whether you think you can or think you can't, either ways you are always right.
> —Henry Ford

"And if you still want more evidence," Harry said, "take a look at what some scriptures have to say," another slide appeared.

You are what your deep, driving desire is
As your desire is, so is your will
As your will is, so is your deed
As your deed is, so is your destiny.

—Upanishad

All that we are is a result of what we have thought.

—Buddha

And all things, whatsoever ye ask in prayer, believing, ye shall receive.

—Matthew 21:22

What things so ever ye desire, when ye pray, believe that ye receive them, and ye shall have them.

—Mark 11:24

Ask, and it shall be given you; seek, and ye shall find; knock, and it shall be opened unto you

—Mathew 7:7

The lady was startled and impressed by the amount of evidence Harry had immediately offered. I couldn't help but appreciate the scope of his wisdom.

"Will you please guide us on how to change our attitude towards money?" another participant asked.

"I am going to do just that," Harry said, "remember the circle I showed you yesterday? The one where all the elements began with 'S'? Two points were still left to be discussed. Does anyone remember those points?"

"Scarcity and stinginess!" we replied.

"That's correct. We will discuss a few steps by which you can create a positive blueprint and attract more money in your life. Let's begin with scarcity first. When we were young, our elders hammered our subconscious with negative statements like, 'Money is so difficult to earn', 'You think money grows on trees?', 'Go out in the world and you will see how difficult it is to earn money'.

"Listening to such statements over and over again forces us to develop a scarcity mentality. We start believing that there is too little in the world and we must struggle to earn money in order to survive. The Universe reflects this attitude and aptly creates more and more scarcity in our lives.

"Why do you think that with each day, the rich keep getting richer and the poor continue to attract more and more poverty? You think it is an accident. No, it is bound to be that way. The rich understand something that the poor do not. The poor have a scarcity mentality which is why they experience a lack of everything. The rich have an abundance mentality which is why they have everything in sufficient quantities."

Harry told us that one-fourth of humanity is dying due to poverty and hunger. Millions of others struggle for an entire lifetime because of the illusion that one day they will own a dream house or car, which always eludes them. However, the whole of mankind needs a 'paradigm shift', from a scarcity mentality to one of abundance. The world needs to know that there is enough on the planet for everybody's needs. If all the assets in the world were to be equally divided by the entire population on the globe, each one of us would have a wonderful house, a wonderful car, and enough money and resources to last a lifetime.

"There is a very interesting statement in the Bible which I read a few days ago," Harry said, gesturing to Saloni to get the book. She walked towards him holding out the Bible.

"I have a copy of the New Testament with me," he started looking for the right page. "Here it is, in Matthew 25:29. It says, 'For to every person who has something, even more will be given, and he will have more than enough; but the person who has nothing, even the little that he has will be taken away from him'.

"At first read it sounds unbelievable. The Bible is saying that those who have been blessed with resources, more will be given to them! And those who have not been blessed with resources, whatever little they have will be taken away!

"But this has to be understood in a certain context," he added. "The Bible tells us a story, called 'The Parable of the Three Servants'. There was once a man who had three servants. Before departing on a long journey, he called his three servants and handed them 5000, 2000, and 1000 gold coins, as per their abilities. The master left. Meanwhile, the servants who had received 5000 and 2000 gold coins, invested the money and in time it doubled. While the servant who had 1000 gold coins was afraid of losing the money if he invested it, and hence dug a hole in the ground. When the master came back, he was happy with the first two servants who had doubled his money by investing it, but he was really upset with the third servant. He took away the 1000 gold coins as punishment, and gave it to the first servant as a reward for wise thinking."

Harry closed the Bible and gave it back to Saloni. "This incident is just a parable, but there is a deep meaning behind the story. The first two servants operated from an abundance mentality. They did not mind parting with the money and investing it, but the third servant had a scarcity mentality. He preferred keeping the money with himself and therefore he made nothing of his share.

"In real life too you will notice the same phenomena. As time passes by, the rich keep on getting richer and the poor get poorer. The rich somehow tend to attract opportunities that bless them with more wealth, while the poor tend to attract natural calamities, illnesses, accidents, and death which will erode all their savings.

"Observe the domestic help working in your home and you will be surprised to notice that whenever he gets money from you he somehow tends to attract some critical illness or unexpected accident in his family that erodes all the wealth. However much he earns, money does not stay with him. Ultimately, he develops a firm belief that he is unlucky and starts cribbing about wealth. Little do such people realise that it is precisely this mentality of cribbing and complaining about money that washes away all their wealth.

"Do not believe that your wealth reserves are like a pond," Harry stressed, "instead believe that your wealth is like an ocean. A pond has limited capacity, but an ocean is infinite.

"Haven't we all seen people who will keep on wearing the same old shoes till the sole gets worn out, or those who squeeze the toothpaste tube till the last drop is utilised? What are these people doing? Unconsciously, they are sending a message to their mind that money is scarce and so they must make full use of their resources. But, rich people generally don't show such miserly behaviour. You may argue that 'they are rich, therefore they don't need to compromise'. But the truth is the other way around, 'because they don't compromise, they are rich'.

"In Hindu mythology, Goddess Lakshmi is the Goddess of Wealth. Look at any of her paintings and you will see her wearing a bright garment and sparkling gold ornaments. Around her there will be expensive objects studded with precious stones. You will never see Goddess Lakshmi in tattered clothes or unpolished jewellery. The message is clear. The Goddess of Wealth loves luxury. Do not settle for anything substandard. Instead opt for a comfortable lifestyle."

Many participants including me were finding Harry's words extremely lethal. He was literally peeling off layers and layers of negative notions that we had been holding for years.

"We now come to the last 'S'— 'Stinginess'! But, before I go ahead I want to know how many of you habitually give missed calls to people?"

Everybody raised their hands. All of us were laughing for we knew what he was trying to say.

"If it solves your purpose, it's fine. But, some people make this a regular habit. Even when it is their work that needs to be done, they will give you a missed call and expect you to call them back.

"I have seen some people who have even designed a code for the calls," Harry added. "If they give one missed call, then the answer is yes. If they give two missed calls, the answer is no, and so on."

I could see everyone around me nod and smile.

"You may save a few bucks every month," Harry said with a very serious expression, "but every time you resort to such stinginess, you are sending a signal to your brain that 'money is less' and like an obedient genie it responds by creating financial constraints in your life.

"When I was in college I used to do the same thing. During dinner with friends, I would excuse myself and go to the washroom just before the bill was presented. I never wanted to pay. It was extremely painful for my mind to give something away; all I believed in was receiving.

"Later, when I met rich people and observed their lifestyle, I learnt two very powerful lessons that I want to share with you. First, *'you can become a little rich by saving on expenses, but to be super rich, you must focus on increasing your revenue'.*

"And second, *'people do not remain poor because of their inability to earn. They remain poor because of their unwillingness to spend, which restricts their ability to earn!'*"

He told us that the whole world needs a 'paradigm shift'. Instead of encouraging stinginess, one must be encouraged to spend and give away wealth whenever it is necessary and required. Even the word 'currency' came from the word 'current'. Like a river current, money must constantly flow in and out of your life. If you are blocking the outflow of money, you are blocking the inflow.

Prophet Muhammad had even made it obligatory for rich Muslims to give away a certain percentage of their wealth. And whenever one gave, he was supposed to give with humility and love, not with grudge or after being forced.

"You will be surprised to know that the world's richest people are also the world's greatest givers. People like Bill Gates and Warren Buffet have given away large portions of their wealth, yet surprisingly they never get poor. The more they give, the more money comes to them. Why does this happen? Because, whenever they are giving, they are sending a signal to their mind, 'Don't worry, by giving away I will not become poor. Money will easily come to me'. And like an obedient genie, the Universe says, 'Your wish is my command', and generates wealth for them.

"When Dhirubhai's business had started flourishing in Mumbai, he would occasionally have his evening coffee at Taj Hotel. A cup of coffee was priced at Rs. 65, a lot of money in those days. Dhirubhai's friends from his village thought he had gone mad. Such habits would ruin him and his company. But Dhirubhai's attitude was different. By insisting on a premium lifestyle, he was telling his mind that he deserved to have the best, and the mind responded by giving him the best in life.

"In those days, most companies were so stingy that they never gave adequate dividends to shareholders. But Ambani was generous in his offerings. He always gave more than the investors expected. The proprietors of other companies thought this would reduce his wealth but in reality, the exact opposite happened. Since he had the blueprint of a rich man, the more Dhirubhai gave, the richer he became!"

Harry told us that many people have this tendency of

buying things only when the need for it arises. "They will tell you, 'Why should I spend money on applying for a passport. Anyway I am never going to go abroad', or they will tell you, 'Why should I book a garage in my building. Anyway I am never going to buy a car'.

"In reality, because of such confirmed justifications they are actually blocking foreign visits and cars from coming into their life. A better strategy would be to acquire things in advance with a clear intention that you will need and use them. This will go a long way in fulfilling your dreams.

"We discussed the shift from 'scarcity' to 'abundance' and from 'stinginess' to 'generosity'. Now we will do the last shift, from 'subconscious' to 'conscious'.

"The other day someone gifted me a copy of a wonderful book called *I Love Money*. On the cover, the author has written a very important statement. He says, 'When you pay attention to money, it grows!'

"The problem with our education system is that there is lot of emphasis on academic literacy, but very little emphasis on financial literacy. We teach our children the history of dead people and the geographical topography of irrelevant places, but we will never teach them the fundamental principles of handling wealth. The result? We have so many highly educated people who are constantly in debt.

"Just five minutes ago I told you how Dhirubhai used to have coffee in a five star hotel. But there was a certain context behind that example. If you try to imitate him blindly, you'll go bust!

"Ambani was a mastermind as far as finance was concerned. You would be surprised to know that for the first 30 years of its existence, Reliance was a zero-tax company! Every time the government changed a ruling, Dhirubhai would adjust his plans accordingly. Ultimately, after nearly three decades of being dodged, the government was forced to introduced a 'minimum alternate tax' plan which compelled every corporate enterprise to pay a minimum tax, no matter what the circumstance.

"'Money is power'," Harry declared, "if you use it properly, it will bless your life. But if you use it incorrectly, it will ruin you.

"When I say one has to be 'conscious' about money, I mean one has to make all possible attempts to learn and understand the dynamics of handling wealth. Instead of imitating the wealthy people blindly, one must learn the ways by which they create wealth.

"Take a stroll outside our centre and you will find many people talking about the stock market and which companies to invest in. Yet, not even five percent of them would have bothered to study the track record or the price-earnings ratio of the company in which they are putting their money."

Harry told us that he did not want us to be money-minded, but definitely wanted us to be money-conscious.

"Tomorrow, I will teach you the Second Secret Law of Money. But, I would like to end today's session with a real life story on how 'money is a manifestation of our mentality'.

"Many of you must have heard of Jack Canfield, author of the international bestseller *Chicken Soup for the Soul*. Well, as the story goes, Jack wanted to be a millionaire, but had no clue on how he would do it. But, having read the biographies of many rich people, he knew that money is a manifestation of one's mentality. He knew the required money could be materialised. So he created a dummy cheque and wrote the amount $1,000,000 and hung it on the ceiling of his bedroom. Every morning, the first thing he saw was the cheque. He would close his eyes and visualise that the cheque was real and he was holding it in his hand. Then he would visualise all the things he could do with the million dollars.

"Interestingly, a few days later, a helpful coincidence shaped his life. He met a reporter and while talking with her, Jack was suddenly reminded of an unpublished manuscript that he had written a few months ago. The lady helped him publish the book which became an instant hit. Within a week, tens of thousands of copies were sold and it climbed to the *New York Times* #1 Bestselling List. For months it stayed there generating massive royalties for Jack. And believe it or not, at the end of the year, Jack received a $1,000,000 cheque from his publisher!

"It was the only time his publisher had ever issued a $1,000,000 to someone!"

If you live the right mentality as an actuality, it becomes reality!

———

THE BEST AND THE WORST THING TO HAPPEN TO SOMEONE IS TO KNOW THAT IT'S ALL IN ONE'S OWN HANDS!

—AKANKSHA THAKORE

Every night, after listening to Harry, I only found faults in myself, or blamed myself for my inadequacies. I think it had become habitual. I was enjoying the misery. But, an important lesson I learnt that day was that 'our thoughts create our world'. This meant if one entertained negative thoughts for a long time, he, or she, would attract negative circumstances in life, and the circle continues.

Therefore, that night I decided not to criticise myself, but to simply 'feel good' and positive about who I was.

I was reminded of an example Harry had given that day. "Have you ever seen a bumblebee?" he had asked. "A bumblebee has a very heavy body and relatively tiny wings. From the viewpoint of physics, a bumblebee cannot fly. Its wings are too delicate to lift up its body. However, the bumblebee does not know physics. Its mental blueprint is full of possibility and hence it just keeps on flying!

"Even ants can lift about 50 times their body weight.

No other creature in the world can do this. Science says it's virtually impossible. But, ants don't know science and so they just carry on.

"Quite similarly, if one develops the attitude of a winner and refuses to entertain negative thoughts, nothing in the world can stop him from advancing!"

THE SECOND SECRET
LAW OF MONEY

"For many years, it was always believed that the earth is the centre of the solar system, and not the sun." Harry initiated a new session. "But Copernicus presented a new theory, he said that the sun is the centre of the solar system, and not the earth. When people heard this they thought Copernicus had gone mad.

"In fact, many years later, when Galileo proclaimed that it's the earth that revolves around the sun and not vice versa, people considered him a big fool. The Church was infuriated to such an extent that it ostracised Galileo. It was not that Galileo did not present scientific evidence to support his theory, but people were so obsessed with their set beliefs that they did not bother to check the facts that he had presented. However, once it was established that Galileo's research was indeed authentic, it opened new dimensions in the field of astronomy.

"Quite similarly," Harry said, "We all have a set belief about money which is very difficult to change. Ever since we were little, we heard our elders tell us, 'One must work hard to earn money', 'the higher your efforts, the higher your income'. But the second secret law of money says exactly the opposite. It says," and the words appeared on the screen.

IF YOU WANT TO GET RICH, YOU MUST NEVER WORK FOR MONEY. INSTEAD, YOU MUST MAKE MONEY WORK FOR YOU!

"It is quite natural that when you hear this statement, you won't feel like believing it. Even Galileo and Copernicus fought all their life to convince people to change their perceived notions. But, tell you what," Harry promised, "once you get this 'shift', you will be able to create wealth with absolute ease and without effort!

"In our discussion today, I will teach you not one, but three different models by which you can create income effortlessly. Here they are," he clicked and a new slide appeared.

- LEVERAGING
- COMPETENCY
- REPLICATION

Honestly speaking, we were all blank about where this session was headed. First of all, it was difficult to believe that one could earn money as easily as Harry claimed. Secondly, the three words hardly made any sense.

"Let us begin with 'Leveraging'," Harry seemed to be unfazed by the confusion on our faces.

"If you look around, you will find that most of the people are following the 'time for money' model. They are giving their time and in return they are being paid money; say for example, a daily worker in a factory. Every day he goes to work and based on the number of hours he spends there, he is given a certain salary. Dhirubhai too started his career along similar lines. For about eight years, he worked with Burmah Shell before finally quitting work and plunging into entrepreneurship. I, too, worked with Reliance during the early days of my career and then moved on to an MNC before finally quitting work and starting Om Group. Sometime during the last year of work as an employee, my Bania instincts urged me to quit the 'time for money' model and start leveraging.

"Now, the obvious question is what is this 'time for money' model and what is 'leveraging', but before I explain these terms, I want to know whether anybody has read the book *Rich Dad Poor Dad* by Robert Kiyosaki."

A couple of hands were raised.

"It's an awesome book and I especially like it because the author has explained leveraging with a simple, yet powerful, story.

"In a village there were two young boys who had big dreams, but were unemployed. One day, the village chief summoned them and asked if they would like to do some work. 'We need people to fetch water from a nearby village,' the chief said, 'for every bucket you carry, you will be paid a cent.'

"Both boys were overjoyed and accepted the offer right away. Every day they would set out with buckets in each hand and carry back the water to the village. Days went by and they started carrying more and more water to the village. Their income increased and so did their savings. Somewhere down the line, one of the boys realised that bucket carrying was a tedious job. Carrying heavy buckets was painful work. They were making lots of money, and they had to continue doing this, if they wanted the income. If they stopped, their income would cease. So, one of the boys decided to build a pipeline from the stream to the village tank. He shared the idea with the other boy, but the latter didn't like it.

'Once the pipeline is built, the water will flow on its own without us having to carry it,' the first boy reasoned.

'But we are so busy carrying buckets, we don't have time to build the pipeline,' the other boy argued.

"The second boy was worried that he would have to forego his current cash flow for some future uncertainty.

"So the first boy started building the pipeline all by himself. He would carry buckets on weekdays and use his free time to build the pipeline on weekends. The villagers mocked him for wasting time on what they perceived was a stupid idea. But, the boy did not pay attention, and continued his hard work. For many weekends, he worked hard and ultimately the pipeline was built.

'Phew!' he sighed as he placed the last brick. 'Now I can afford to relax and yet money will flow in,' he thought.

"Sure enough, the water started flowing through the pipeline and his profits started increasing. He didn't carry buckets anymore, and yet his income continued to flow. When he was asleep, his income flowed. When he was on vacation, his income flowed. Instead of him working for the system, now the system worked for him. Meanwhile, his friend, who had started using bigger buckets to earn more money developed stooped shoulders and was exhausted carrying water. The pipeline fulfilled the villagers' requirements and he was now unemployed!

"This story was originally mentioned by Robert Kiyosaki," Harry said, "but Burke Hedges, another author, goes one step further and says that the boy did not stop after building his first pipeline. He decided to build pipelines for all nearby villages and cities, and also sell the idea in different parts of the world. On every project he would earn and soon the income increased because of the hundreds of thousands of pipelines he was now building, millions of dollars flowed to him."

"Yes, yes, I remember this story," Abhi whispered. "Our professor in IIM had told us this."

"What Dhirubhai did, and later I used the same strategy, was that once we had enough savings we switched from the 'time for money' model and started making pipelines. In other words, we ceased working for others and started building our personal cash flows. Carrying buckets is safe and secure since immediate income is assured, but for that you have to constantly exchange 'time for money'.

"Take for example a craftsman who offers his services for Rs. 100 an hour. He gives you 'one hour of his time' and in exchange demands Rs. 100 of your wealth. On an average day, if he works for eight hours, how much will his income be?"

"Rs. 800," we responded.

"Correct. But that will be the upper limit. He cannot earn more. And sometimes if he works double shifts, he will earn Rs. 1600, but not more. So although the time for money model is good, there is a limit to your earnings because we all have limited time at our disposal. And if you don't work on holidays, or when you are sick, after your retirement your income becomes zero. But, your expenses will continue, leading to an erosion of your savings.

"On the other hand, if you build a pipeline, you don't have to permanently exchange time for money. Yes, it will require sacrificing both time and money initially, but once the pipeline is built, you can enjoy effortless income forever. Whether you devote any further time to it, or not, your income will continue to flow. And the biggest benefit is that when you die, even your children can inherit the income pipeline. So, the income will outlive you and benefit several generations.

"Let us take a look at this chart, and you will see how the leveraging model scores over the 'time for money' model.

TIME FOR MONEY MODEL (Active Income)	LEVERAGING MODEL (Passive Income)
Ongoing exchange of time for money	Exchange time once, earn money forever
Requires physical presence	Works even in your absence
Doesn't work when you are asleep	Works when you are asleep
You work for the system	The system works for you
Cannot be inherited	Can be inherited
Depend on someone else	You are your own boss
Physically tiring and demanding	Requires initial efforts, but effortless thereafter

"I have a practical problem on leveraging, but am not sure if I should give it to you or not. Would you like to solve it?

"Yes," we said immediately.

"All right then. Let's make this discussion more enriching. I will give you a case study based on which I will ask you a few questions. As soon as you get the answer, just speak up. Don't wait for me to find you."

Harry signalled to his assistants to distribute a few worksheets. I received mine and it had a case study on leveraging. I asked Abhi to help me, he was better at handling such problems.

"Let's begin," Harry had the worksheet in his hand. "I will read the problem given to you and then we will proceed towards the questions."

"Please note that this is just a hypothetical example," he pointed out. "Leveraging is a more complex term and will take some time to understand. But, for the time being, this example will suffice."

"Mr. Jain owns a watch business in Kolkata," he started reading. "He manufactures about 5000 watches a month and the production is outsourced to five contractors, each of whom is required to produce 1000 watches. Each contractor in turn has 10 labourers under him who produce 100 watches each. Mr. Jain pays Rs. 150 to the contractor for each watch produced, of which the contractor takes Rs. 50 as profit and pays Rs. 100 to the labourer. Raw material is irrelevant and will be ignored. Mr. Jain's profit is Rs. 25 per watch.

"Now I will give you five minutes. You tell me what the monthly income of Mr. Jain is, and of the contractors, and labourers."

"Abhi," I said, pen and paper ready. "I will do the calculations. You just tell me whether I am right or wrong."

"Okay"

"Hmm...first let us begin with the labourers. One labourer makes 100 watches and for each watch he gets Rs. 100, so his income is Rs. 10,000. Right?"

"Right."

"Good. Now, let's go to the contractor. His income would be 100 watches by one labourer multiplied by 10 such labourers multiplied by..."

"Rs. 50 per watch," Abhi completed. "That would be Rs. 50,000."

"And Mr. Jain's income is Rs. 25 per watch, multiplied by five contractors, multiplied by 10 labourers multiplied by 100 watches each. So it is...."

"You can directly take 5000 watches into 25," Abhi suggested, "that would be Rs. 1,25,000."

"Oh yes, that would be easier to calculate."

I drew a neat table for the answers.

LABOURER	WORKS CONTRACTOR	OWNER
Rs. 100 x 100 watches = *Rs. 10,000*	Rs. 50 x 10 labourers x 100 watches = *Rs. 50,000*	Rs. 25 x 5000 watches = *Rs. 1,25,000*

Harry was walking down the aisle glancing at people's

notebooks. After a few minutes, he asked us to stop.

"All right, that's enough of calculations," he said. "Let's take a look at the correct answers," he clicked for the next slide on the screen.

EFFORTS		INCOME	
Labourer	Highest	Labourer	10,000
Contractor	Medium	Contractor	50,000
Mr. Jain	Lowest	Mr. Jain	125,000

We tallied our answers with his. Almost everybody had got it right.

"Tell me, who puts in the highest efforts in making the watches?"

"The labourer."

"And the lowest?"

"Mr. Jain."

"But, who has the highest overall income?"

"Mr. Jain."

"And the lowest?"

"The labourer."

"So, is there a direct relationship between the efforts and rewards, or an inverse relationship?"

"Inverse!"

"Good," Harry smiled, "take a look at this chart."

	EFFORTS	LEVERAGING	INCOME
Labourer	Highest	Lowest	Lowest
Contractor	Medium	Medium	Medium
Mr. Jain (Owner)	Lowest	Highest	Highest

"It can be easily verified from the chart" Harry inferred, "that *the amount of money a person earns, is not proportionate to the efforts he puts in; it is proportionate to the leveraging he does!*"

"But what exactly is 'leveraging'? I am still confused," a participant said.

"'Leveraging' comes from the word 'lever'," Harry explained. "Remember the see-saw on which you used to play during childhood — that is like a lever.

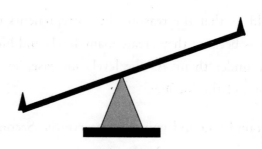

"In a lever, when one end goes down, the other end comes up. So in leveraging, you profit by making a person or system work for you. Like in the example we just discussed, the labourer has zero leverage. The contractor leverages on the efforts of the labourers while Mr. Jain leverages on the efforts of all the contractors and labourers. Observe this chart:

INCOME PER WATCH	
Labourer	100
Contractor	50
Mr. Jain (Owner)	25

"The income per watch is highest for a labourer but he can only earn from the watches that he manufactures. The contractor, on the other hand, has lesser income per watch as compared to the labourers, but he leverages on the income of 10 such labourers, and increases his final earnings. And the owner, although he has the least income per watch, leverages on the income of all the contractors, multiplied by all the labourers under each contractor, and hence his income is the highest."

Harry told us that the reason why entrepreneurs earn lots of money is because they create many levels and hierarchies of people under them. As the levels increase, so does the leveraging and the income.

"Look around you and you will observe the Second Secret

Law of Money at work. At a construction site, the worker who carries heavy bricks and stones through the day is paid a meagre wage, but the property owner who sits in a comfortable room, earns more than him. In a restaurant, the waiter and cook slog through the day to get just basic remuneration, and the boss who relaxes at the cash counter gets to earn stacks of cash every day. Those who work for others earn less; but those who leverage on the efforts of others, earn more.

"But, leveraging can only be done by businessmen," someone objected.

"Not necessary. Even employees leverage on the efforts of each other. In the corporate world, the top management leverages on the senior manager's efforts, who leverages on the junior manager's efforts. As the hierarchy rises, so does leveraging and salaries."

Harry asked for a chair. He looked a little tired. After asking us a few general questions to check whether we had understood what he had said, he moved ahead.

"The next model is called 'Competency'. You have already heard the word 'Competency' before, when was it?"

"When you were discussing 'Being', the first circle," an alert participant replied immediately.

"That's correct. 'Competency' is related to 'Being'. As your competency increases, two things happen simultaneously – your efforts decrease and your income increases! Look at this graph," we all looked at the screen.

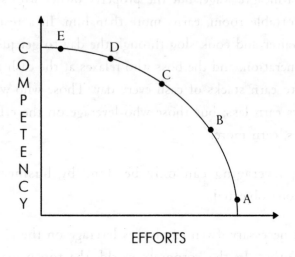

"On the horizontal axis we have plotted 'Efforts' and on the vertical axis, we have plotted 'Competency'. Between the axes we have shown a performance curve, where different points A, B, C, D, and E are plotted.

"Look at point A," he said. "We all begin our careers here. Since we have very little competency, skill, or experience, lots of efforts are needed to stay on the performance curve. But as our competency increases, we move to points B, C, and D, in succession. Point E is the highest point in the performance curve. It is that point where your efficiency is so high that you need to put the bare minimum efforts to get things done.

"An important thing to remember here is that although every professional starts his career at point A, most of

them are only able to reach this region," he said indicating
the area between points B and C. "Some people are able to
reach the area near point D. But only a few are able to
reach point E, which is the region of highest competency
and effortlessness. Such people are normally called
'Legends', 'Geniuses', 'Experts', and 'Pros'. People like
Oprah Winfrey, Michael Phelps, The Beatles, Christiano
Ronaldo, Beethoven, Sachin Tendulkar, A. R. Rahman, and
others like them fall in this category. These people don't
demand wealth, they command it. Wherever they go,
money follows them. At times, their professional charges
are many times more than their colleagues, yet we are
willing to pay the price they command. So, if we were to
include a third element called money, this is how the graph
would look," we looked at the screen again.

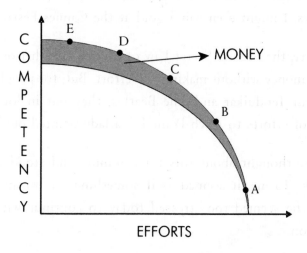

"Professionals who are at point A earn very little money.
Their earnings keep on increasing as their abilities

increase. Professionals, who have reached the highest competency, earn the maximum and that too with effortless ease. A. R. Rahman doesn't have to struggle to compose a good song, he can do it without effort. Sir Don Bradman never struggled to score centuries, it came quite naturally."

I was trying to connect this model to my own life. When I began my career in an advertising agency, I used to struggle to write scripts. Perhaps, I was at point A then, because even my salary was very low. But, in the last two years, my experience and income had increased. Now I could script a story quickly. At times, I didn't struggle at all. The work had become regular, and so the script came quite naturally to me. I think I was at Point C. Someday, maybe when I would further increase my competency to level E, who knows, I might even win a gold at the Cannes Festival!

"Harry, the Second Secret Law of Money says that one can earn money without making any effort. But, for people like Sachin Tendulkar and The Beatles, they put in lots and lots of efforts to reach Point E," a lady pointed out.

Harry thought about this for a minute and stood up to speak. To me, it seemed as if something was wrong with him; he seemed too stressed today to continue with the session.

"Yes, it is true that they put in efforts. But, money only came to them only when they were in the 'effortless zone'.

This area between points D and E," Harry pointed out, "as long as they were putting in efforts at points A and B, there was very little money in their life."

"Okay, got it!" the lady nodded.

"And secondly," Harry explained, "to an outsider, it might appear as if they are still making efforts, but 'geniuses' are madly passionate about the work they do. Sachin never considered practising cricket as an effort, he loved it! The Beatles were crazy about their music, and so on."

Harry explained that as our competency increases, the sky is the limit as far as money is concerned. In the business world, entrepreneurs struggled to keep their prices low to increase demand. But in the world of competency, there was no such thing. Someone like Will Smith who charged a few million dollars to act in a film would always find work rather than the hundreds of other struggling actors in Hollywood who were ready to work at one-tenth or one-hundredth of that amount. *Where there is competency, there is no competition!*

"We now come to the last and final model for the day — 'Replication'. We have discussed the Playground theory in which all the elements began with 'P'. We have also discussed another theory where all the elements began with 'S'. Now, we will discuss a theory that tells you how to earn unlimited income by using four different elements, each beginning with 'R'. They are Rent, Royalty, Rights, and Returns, and are part of my '7R theory'. Look at this diagram."

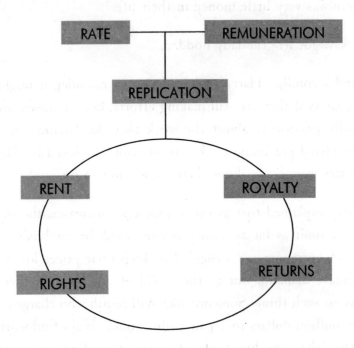

"Prior to the industrial revolution, production was manual. There were no big machines that could automatically manufacture goods. Society was divided into two — those who dealt in goods, and those who dealt in services. Though both dealt with different elements, their earnings were more or less similar. Goods were sold for a 'rate' and services were offered for 'remuneration'.

"So, if I purchased bread from a baker what would I give him?"

"The rate," we answered instantly.

"Correct. And if I asked a chef to cook for me, what would I give?"

"Remuneration!"

"Perfect."

"So society was made up of only two 'R's. Rate, for those who offered goods, and remuneration for those who offered services. These were the two primary forms of income.

"However, with the Industrial Revolution, something extraordinary happened. Machines made it possible to 'Replicate' goods in mass quantities. People suddenly realised that instead of working for money, they could make their machines earn for them! It was a 'life-altering' insight. 'If it is possible to generate passive income, why work hard earning active income' they thought.

"Since then, four amazing ways of earning passive income have evolved. Here they are."

RENT	ROYALTY	RIGHTS	RETURNS

"These four avenues for generating income, are what I call passive incomes. They are based on the 'Replication' model. The more a person builds on these passive income streams, the more effortless wealth he will create for himself.

"And yes, as I said before, no school, college, or university will teach you these techniques. They aren't mentioned in any other book on wealth ever written. We have researched these techniques especially for our training sessions. So let us study them in detail," the next slide appeared on the screen.

"The first is 'Rent'. It is a traditional form of income which you and I are pretty familiar with. If I give my property on lease to somebody, he will pay 'rent'. This is my additional income. I don't have to give up my time and labour to earn it. My property earns for me. I am not consciously putting in any effort.

"Moreover, since the possession of the property remains with me, I get two more benefits. First, the ever rising property prices will increase its value as an asset and secondly, I can even mortgage my property to get loans."

Harry told us how multitudes of smart investors were using this concept to 'replicate' their income. They would lease an asset to earn rent and re-invest the rent amount in purchasing more assets, which would generate even higher amounts of rent.

"The second type of passive income is Royalty. It is a rare but wonderful form of passive income.

"By the way, do you know who the richest lady in UK is?" Harry asked.

Richest lady in UK? I thought, could it be the Queen?

"Is it the Queen?" I asked Harry.

"I knew someone would say that, but I am afraid you are wrong."

He looked around if anyone else had the answer ready, but everyone looked blank. Forbes normally featured men and therefore they were more famous. Guessing a woman's name was relatively tougher.

"It's J. K. Rowling," Harry disclosed finally, "the lady who created Harry Potter. From humble beginnings she has become the world's richest celebrity. Not because she is the CEO of an MNC or the heiress of a rich billionaire, but because she took advantage of 'Royalty'.

"Her books on Harry Potter have sold more than 325 million copies in over 65 languages. The only effort that Rowling puts in, is writing the manuscripts in English. After that it's the publisher's headache. For every copy of the book that is sold in English, Rowling gets the royalty. Further, every time her book is translated in another language, she gets additional royalty without any effort! Since her books have been translated in 65 languages, it's like 65 cash-pipelines continuously pouring wealth into her cash-tub. When its night in UK, its daytime in Australia. So even when she is sleeping, somewhere in some part of the world, people are buying her books and her income continues to flow.

"On witnessing the popularity of Harry Potter, Warner

Brothers paid her millions to make films based on her characters. Next, leading toy manufacturer, Mattel, paid her a few millions for the rights to make toys based on her characters. Then, Electronic Arts, a digital game making company paid Rowling a few hundred thousand dollars to make games based on Harry Potter. Now they are planning to make a theme park in USA based on the Harry Potter series. By putting the Second Secret Law at work, Rowling created a system by which money would come to her rather than her going out to seek it."

"Now I realise why people like Britney Spears and Madonna make so much money," I told Abhi. "It's royalty at work."

"Yes, the only effort involves singing in a recording studio. Then the millions of CDs that are sold worldwide, give them royalty," Abhi replied.

"Friends, I would now like to introduce you to Mr. Khan," Harry said, calling out to a gentleman sitting in the front row. "He is an old acquaintance and runs his own film production company. Mr. Khan will tell you how he capitalised on royalty."

A tall and lanky man rose from his seat and walked on to the stage. Harry handed over the microphone to him.

"Well, before I begin I would like to thank Harry for the wonderful advice he gave me many years ago. Had it not been for his timely insights, I would have still been struggling with my finances."

"And I want to thank you for sparing out time from your busy schedule and coming here," Harry acknowledged. "Please share your story with us."

"Well, you see," Mr Khan began, "about seven years ago, I owned a theatre production group. We used to perform plays in several different locations across the country. But there was an inherent defect in our model. Since theatre necessitates the physical presence of people, every time we had to earn, we had to perform. The day we did not perform, our income was zero."

"And moreover," Harry added, "their only source of income was the sale of tickets," he started drawing a chart on the board.

Income Sources Before Replication	Income Sources After Replication
Ticket Sales	

"That's true; we had only one source of income. But a chance meeting with Harry made me realise that there was tremendous scope of replication in my business model. It was just that we hadn't capitalised on it. Keeping his words in mind, I sat with my team and we brainstormed on how we could change our business model. The very first thing we did was that we took our most popular play and performed it in front of a video camera like they do for films. Then we recorded the whole thing on DVD and sold the video rights to a distribution company. This was the first big leap towards replication. Now, instead of us roaming from city to city and performing, people in any part of the world could simply buy our DVD, play it and make us perform any number of times! They could even pause, rewind and fast forward!" Mr. Khan laughed, "Every DVD sold gave us royalty. Next, we took our popular audio tracks and made an audio CD. This too was distributed like the DVDs to earn royalty. Someone suggested that we give our audio tracks as ringtones for mobile phones. 'Why not?' I said and grabbed the opportunity. We tied up with a leading mobile content distributor. Every time people downloaded one of our ringtones, it would give us income! Some private TV channels approached us and paid us money to air the film based on our play via satellite. We also created an e-store on the Internet and offered our film to be downloaded after e-payment. The Internet is a wonderful platform for leveraging," Mr. Khan opined, "we just uploaded a single file and whenever someone paid to download it, it increased our bank balance. Ever since we started 'replicating', this extra income continues to flow. Just last week a Germany-based theatre company acquired rights for the German translation of our play. That single deal made me richer by $20,000."

"And you didn't have to put in any extra effort for that!" Harry added. "They just took your English DVD and dubbed it in German."

"That's true. And we are also negotiating rights with a leading publisher to make a book based on the drama script."

"Excellent!" Harry laughed. "So this is how your income model looks now," he said writing something in the chart.

Income Sources Before Replication	Income Sources After Replication
Ticket Sales	• Ticket Sales
	• Video DVDs
	• Audio CDs
	• Mobile Downloads
	• Television Broadcast
	• Internet Downloads
	• Language Translations
	• Territory Rights
	• Publishing Royalty

"Originally, you had only one cash pipeline, but now you have many pipelines that continue to fill your cash-tub."

"Yes, and honestly speaking," Mr. Khan turned to us, "now I have made so much money that we will soon be producing frontline Bollywood movies."

"That's awesome," Harry said, "many people have consulted me, but few have implemented my advice the way Mr. Khan has."

We all applauded Mr. Khan for his endeavours.

Harry continued from where Mr. Khan had left off. He

said that the Internet was one of the greatest tools of replication. A local retailer could only sell his products to the people around him, but by opening an e-store, one could sell products in any part of the world. Further, operating an e-store didn't require maintaining any inventory, as a single file could be downloaded infinite times!

"The next way of generating passive income is by 'Rights'. The other day I told you about Ray Croc and McDonalds, when we were discussing 'Efficiency'. Many people think that Ray Croc was the founder of McDonalds, but that is not true. The first ever McDonalds restaurant was started by two brothers Dick and Mac. Croc was merely a supplier and a friend of the brothers, but he was convinced that McDonalds was a brand worth capitalising on. In 1955 he acquired the first 'franchisee' and later purchased substantial equity in McDonalds. Ever since then, Croc and his successors have been aggressively distributing 'franchisee rights' to restaurateurs all over the world. As of today, they have more than 31,000 franchised and company-owned restaurants.

"McDonald's gives you 'rights' to operate as a franchisee," Harry said, "and in return takes away a certain percentage of your sales. All its restaurants, all over the world, continuously pay a certain percentage of their sales to McDonalds.

"Consider a cash-tub that has 31,000 pipelines

continuously filling it with money! This will give you some idea of how much money they make through their 31,000 stores!"

Harry said that Croc originally followed the 'time for money' model. He used to sell milk-shake making machines. But working all by himself, there was a limit to his income. There was only one pipeline filling his cash-tub. So he capitalised on rights and multiplied his income.

"There are many different ways by which one can give rights. They include Franchisee Rights, Brand Rights, Licensing Rights, amongst many others.

"Do you know that not all the American and European branded goods are manufactured there? Some of them are manufactured by local retailers who use the brand name of the foreign company just because it's well known. For this consideration, they pay fees to the foreign company, for whom this is effortless income."

Harry then began drawing a figure on the board. He drew the structure of a 'two-level' organisation, and below it, he drew the structure of a multi-level organisation.

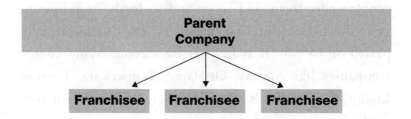

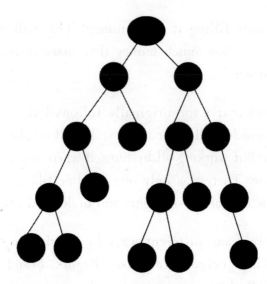

"Let's go back to the example of McDonalds," Harry said. "Croc created, what is called the double level organisation. His company was on top and all franchisees below. But there was a limitation in this model. Croc's franchisees were not allowed to create sub-franchisees. Thus, somewhere in the 1980s some people started thinking of expanding this model and created multiple levels. This was how Multi-Level Marketing was born.

"In a multi-level marketing model," he said pointing towards the diagram in the right "you create a down-line of people under you who create another down-line of people under them, and so on and so forth. As people in your down-line purchase products, the commission is passed on to you. It is like passive income. Many known companies like Amway, Oriflame, Tupperware, Forever Living, Goldquest, RMP, and others are based on this model."

"Is it the same thing as network marketing?" I asked Abhi.

"Yes, they are the same," Abhi replied.

Before ending the discussion on rights, Harry warned us that in the past many multi-level marketing companies had gone bust and looted people of their hard-earned money. So, one had to be extremely cautious before joining any such company.

"We now come to the last element, 'Returns'.

"It is the most common form of effortless income. When you invest your money, you get interest in return. This 'interest' is additional income which you earned without working for it. At times, you even get benefits of capital appreciation. Let's look at some of the ways by which you can earn 'returns'."

- Interest on Loans and Deposits
- Price Appreciation/Bonus/Dividends in Stocks
- Price Appreciation on Property Investments
- Investing in Art & Artifacts
- Investing in Bullion
- Investing in miscellaneous financial schemes

"It may be difficult for a common man to capitalise on Replication, Royalty, or Rights, but earning Returns is relatively easy.

"Did you know that if you had invested Rs. 10,000 in the shares of Wipro in 1970, how much that would be today?

We threw some random figures at Harry, but he said we were not even close.

"Rs. 3000 million!" his eyes shone.

"How else do you think Warren Buffet made so much money? Most of his big bucks have come through compound interest, dividends, and capital appreciation on investments."

Abhi shared some knowledge with me. He said that in 1965, one share of Warren Buffet's company Berkshire Hathaway was around $19, but by the end of the century it was worth $70,000!

"Compounding is a very powerful way of multiplying wealth. Unlike remuneration, which increases arithmetically, by compounding your income you can make it increase geometrically.

"Let me tell you a story. Once upon a time there was a king who had a strong affinity towards chess. He threw an open challenge that if anybody would beat him in the game of chess, he would give that person whatever he asked for, but if the person lost he would be imprisoned for life. One fine day, a mathematician, who was passing by his empire heard's of the king's challenge and accepted it. A game of chess was set out, and both sat down to play. To the king's surprise the mathematician was a brilliant player. A tough game ensued but the king lost. 'I am duty bound by my words,' the king told the mathematician, 'Please tell me what you want.'

'To start with, one grain of rice,' the mathematician replied.

'Just one grain?" the king was startled.

'Well, it would be like this,' the mathematician explained. 'There are 64 squares on the chess board. You will give me one grain of rice for the first square, then double that number and give me two grains for the second square, then double it and give me four grains for the third square and so on..."

"The king was ecstatic. He thought that the mathematician was going to ask for something really big, but instead he was asking for something very trivial.

'Then it will be so,' the king quickly ordered his servants to execute the demand. One servant brought a bag of rice and started placing the grains on the chess board. One grain on the first square, two grains on the second, then four, 8, 16, 32, 64, 128, 256, and so on. By the time he had finished the second line, the whole bag was empty. In fact for the 16th square alone more than 32,000 grains of rice were required. The small bags gave way to medium size bags which gave way to big bags. The 17th square required more than 64,000 grains and the 18th square more than 128,000 grains. Very soon the servants told the king that all the rice in the kitchen was over. The king asked them to fetch more bags from the warehouse, but after filling a few more squares, even that proved insufficient. They had hardly reached halfway across the chess-board when the king realised that all the rice in his kingdom would be insufficient.

"The desperate king bowed to the mathematician and asked him to forgive him. In return he would make him his counsel and bestow him with riches. The mathematician gladly accepted.

"Later, when the king requested the mathematician to explain how he had thought of such an impossible demand, the mathematician explained that to fill the 64th square, the king would have required at least 18 million trillion tonnes of rice grain. This was a dozen times the total quantity of rice in the world!"

Harry's story on compounding reminded me of a poem by Rumi. He had written that nature is miraculous. Everything in nature multiplies by compounding itself. One seed can make the whole earth green!

"So, with this we complete our discussion on Rights and the 7R theory. Remember," Harry said, "Replication is the third powerful tool by which you can enhance your income. It wasn't available prior to the Industrial Revolution. Before the 17th century, if one wanted to make a copy of a book he had to write down every page. It was very cumbersome and tiring. Further, the effort-reward ratio was 1:1. But Gutenberg's printing press made replication possible and it opened up new dimensions for the whole of humanity. Now, one just needed to write a book once and tens of thousands of copies could be produced. The effort-reward ratio changed to 1: Infinite!"

Now, I realised how Bill Gates had become the world's richest man. Initially, he had to spend a lot of time coding his first operating system. But once that was done, he simply kept on replicating his Windows OS, and made millions and millions of copies. Gates would be sleeping at home or holidaying with his family, but in some corner of the world people would be buying his product and generating wealth for him!

"There is a popular story about the Coca Cola company. Many years back, Coca Cola was only available in stores, like the way we have 'Fountain Coke' these days. Every time someone wanted to buy it, he had to go to a store, press the button on the soda machine and the cola would pour through the faucet.

"One day, a man approached the chief of Coca Cola and said that he had a brilliant idea to increase the sales of his company, but he would share it only if the company agreed to pay him $5 million as consultation fees for the idea."

"The chief was hesitant and so a deal was struck. He would pay the consultant only if he implemented the idea, not otherwise."

"And do you know what happened? The consultant whispered just two words to the chief. The latter was so impressed by the idea that he paid the consultant the agreed sum and implemented his idea straightaway!

"Does anybody know what those two words were?"

Nobody knew.

"Bottle it!" Harry said.

"The consultant suggested that Coca Cola be sold in bottles. Thus, instead of people having to go to a store each time they wanted to buy it, they could easily stock bottles at home and drink it at their convenience!

"I don't know how true this story is," Harry accepted, "someone had e-mailed this story to me. But nonetheless, it is a classic example of replication. The millions of bottles that Coca Cola produced after that phenomenally enhanced its sales."

Harry told us that everything in nature is effortless. Grass doesn't try to grow, it just grows. Birds don't attempt to fly, they just fly. Fish don't struggle to swim, they just swim. Quite similarly, we don't need to struggle or work hard to make money. It should come naturally and effortlessly to us.

"Money is like a seed," Harry took another example from nature, "a seed once sown multiplies itself into millions and millions of seeds. The same is with money. Once you invest it, it will keep on compounding and growing."

As we came towards the end of the session, Harry recalled how as a young boy he had lived in extreme poverty. "My father was a nice fellow, but his partners cheated him in business and absconded with his money. He was so shocked with the experience that he suffered from a heart attack and died a few days later. His expensive medical treatment and high hospital bills eroded all of our savings. From a well-to-do family we were reduced to rags in a year's time. When my father was doing well, everybody was friendly, but when calamity stuck, even our near and dear ones deserted us. It was then that I realised a bitter truth – 'Money is a Must'!

"I still remember those days when my mother would avoid taking us through streets where there were toy shops, for the fear that my little sister would fall in love with a doll. We simply couldn't afford it.

"She was a sweet angel. The loveliest gift I ever had. But my sister didn't live long. There was a hole in her heart since she was born. One day she slept and never woke up again. It was all over."

For the first time I saw Harry's face enveloped in sadness. A tear ran down his cheek and he took out a handkerchief to wipe his face.

"I still regret not being able to save the child's life. Many years have gone by but childhood memories cannot be forgotten so easily. Often when I am alone in my room I am gripped by the visions of the sandcastles that we built or the sweet kiss she would give me every night before sleeping.

"Even in those days I was hardworking and efficient. But, like the billions of others on this planet I thought that the only way to earn was by exchanging 'time for money'. I had never heard of Replication, Leveraging, and Competency. If I wanted to earn more I put in more efforts. At times my feet would ache at night, but I suffered the pain silently because some extra money helped in supporting the family.

"Now when I look back, I feel that if somebody had shared this knowledge with me earlier, my life would have been radically different. Perhaps, I would have supported my family better, or been able to afford better medical treatment and saved my sister's life," he said as another tear ran down his cheek.

Harry asked his assistant to get him a glass of water. I suddenly saw that Harry looked very old and vulnerable. He had been speaking for hours, day after day, it must be very tiring. The only thing that kept him going was his desire to make a difference.

"Nevertheless, I am happy that although I didn't get the technology, you got it. Use it to..." Harry suddenly collapsed on the floor with a heavy grunt.

"Oh shucks!" Abhi exclaimed and ran towards the stage.

Many other participants rushed forward.

Harry was semi-conscious. They tried to lift him, but his body had become limp.

Saloni hurried to call the doctor. Within a minute, a few people carrying medical equipment rushed in.

"What happened?" I asked Saloni.

"Well, he had not been keeping well for the past couple of days. But, I never knew it would be this serious," she seemed too numb to speak.

The medical staff carried him away. Thankfully, there was a hospital in our campus.

Everyone was too shocked to do anything. We all gathered together trying to find out what had happened.

Saloni joined us a few minutes later. "Chest pain," she told me, "might be serious. The doctors are still trying to find out. They had advised him not to exert himself. But you see, Harry was desperate to tell you all the three secret laws..."

Oh yes, I said to myself, the third secret law was still left to be discussed. I had forgotten all about it. What if Harry's health turned critical?

No, no, no, it cannot be, I tried to assure myself as we
walked back to our dorms.

Nobody knew what tomorrow would bring...

————

There was no session the next day.

We were told that Harry was fighting for his life. Perhaps, he was not doing it only for himself. Perhaps, he was putting up a fight because he had not reached his goal — teaching us the Third Secret Law. And since he had never discussed it before in public, no participant from a previous batch would be aware of it. This meant that if he didn't live, his last message would forever remain unknown.

All of us waited anxiously for any news. Sameer and the rest of Harry's family flew down from Mumbai. The doctors were trying their best to help him.

Another day passed, without any session. Abhi, all the other participants, and I were extremely anxious. But, late in the night at around 11 pm, when we were just about to turn in for the day, our cellphones beeped simultaneously. It was a message from Saloni — 'Haribhai is recovering slowly, might conduct a seminar tomorrow.'

Both of us heaved a sigh of relief. That was indeed good news!

THE THIRD SECRET LAW OF MONEY

Two people helped Harry get on to the stage. Although he appeared okay, he still looked very weak. He stood for a while and he looked at all of us. When he saw me and Abhi, he smiled at us as if to reassure us that everything was alright.

"How are you feeling Harry?" a girl asked.

"Much better," he smiled. "Thank you for your concern."

He then said, "Nature is very intelligent. It will ensure that its messenger survives all challenges till the message is delivered! The doctors think it is a miracle that I recovered so quickly, but then how else could you have known the Third Secret Law of Money?"

Good old Harry! I whispered to myself, always looking at the positive side. I was indeed happy to see him right in front of my eyes.

"We have already discussed the first two laws of money," he continued, "today, I will tell you the Third Secret Law. But, before we get there I want to tell you something very thought-provoking.

"When the earthquake hit Saroon, thousands of people died. Interestingly, there were very few animals that died.

Just a few seconds before the calamity stuck, most animals sensed impending disaster and rushed towards open spaces.

"Bahadur, our watchman told me, 'That dreaded morning, I was preparing breakfast for myself, when suddenly my dog came rushing to me and started pulling my pant. I could sense that the dog was begging me to follow him somewhere. Out of curiosity, I followed him, and we stepped out of my apartment. No sooner had we moved out of the building, I felt the earthquake. Within seconds, my apartment had crumbled to dust. It was a really narrow escape!'

"Now the question that I want to ask you is, why are animals and birds able to sense natural calamities and not human beings?"

Harry waited for a pretty long time, expecting that someone would respond, but no one did.

"It's because animals live solely by their instincts, while human beings use both instincts as well as intelligence. Look at this," Harry said, while a table appeared on the screen.

ANIMALS	HUMAN BEINGS
Natural Instincts	Natural Instincts & Intelligence

"When an animal feels hungry, it eats food. When it feels thirsty, it drinks water. When it wants to make love, it makes love. When it's time to wake up, it wakes up. When it's time to sleep, it sleeps. Basically, its entire lifestyle is in congruency with its 'natural instincts' therefore it's very easy for it to pick up signals from nature.

"Human beings, on the other hand, do not live by their natural instincts alone. They also consult their own intelligence before making decisions. Even when their body demands food, they will resort to fasting! At times, during the day, they will sleep, and during the night they will work. When an animal wants to make love, it will go ahead and do it. But when a human being wants to make love, he or she will try to suppress that desire. For thousands of years, we have lived a lifestyle that is incongruent with our natural instincts and so we have lost our ability to pick up signals from nature."

"Do you mean to say that we must not use our intelligence?" a participant asked in utter disbelief.

"I never said that. I am only saying that intelligence must be used to enhance our natural instincts, not to go against them.

"Do you know that human beings are the only creatures that suffer from insomnia? Animals rarely, if ever, suffer from lack of sleep. Their life is so well-tuned to their biological clock that sleep comes naturally to them. But, human beings do not follow their natural biological clock. They use their own intelligence to determine when to wake up and when to sleep. It is no wonder that, when we grow old, we require pills and medicines to make us sleep."

Harry told us that human beings are the only creatures in the animal kingdom that suffer from stress, impotency, tension, fatigue, and boredom. Animals almost never experience any of these. Further, only human beings commit suicide, animals never do!

"What an insight!" Abhi said, looking at me to see if I thought so too.

"Terrific!" I agreed.

"You might be wondering why I am telling you all this, instead of teaching you the Third Secret Law. But you see, there is a direct link between the two concepts. The third secret law of money says," he clicked for the next slide.

WHEN PASSION MEETS PROFESSION, MONEY CAN BE MATERIALISED

"Passion in this case means the 'natural instincts' in our hearts and profession means the business, or work that we do. The third law says that when we do what we naturally love to do, we can materialise as much money as we want! Unfortunately, as we just discussed, human beings never live by their natural instincts and that is why we suffer from all types of stress, frustrations and tensions.

"If our heart urges us to pursue a career in acting, we will suppress it and instead take up a career in accounting, because it is more reliable! If our heart urges us to take up photography, we will ignore it and take up management, because it widens our career prospect. Thus, instead of listening to our instincts, we rely more on our intelligence and seek professions that help us survive in this world rather than live a life that we love."

"Excuse me, sir," John, a senior executive, interrupted.

"Yes, John."

"You said that when passion meets profession, money can be materialised. But in my case, even though both my passion and profession are different, yet I make good money."

"I never said you won't make money. I only said that you won't be able to materialise it."

"What's the difference?"

"Making money involves struggling very hard and working for long hours to earn it. You may succeed, but, in the long run, you will get frustrated with life. On the other hand, materialising money involves simply focusing on what you love to do, leaving aside all your concerns about money. Because, if you do what you love to do, money will naturally flow to you. At any point of time you can attract as much money as you want."

"Is this actually possible?" John asked incredulously.

"What are you referring to?"

"That at any point of time one can easily create as much money as he wants," John said in disbelief.

"Yes, provided you marry your passion to your profession. Remember Barbara Pais?" Harry asked, "I told you about her the other day."

"The lady who used to design ads?"

"Yes, the same one. Barbara's passion was creative designing. But professionally, she was employed as an accountant. Every morning, she dragged herself to office, never really enjoying her work. Her boss noticed her lack of enthusiasm and fired her. After unsuccessfully trying for other accounting jobs, she finally gave up."

"Then what happened?"

"Well, as I said, I urged her to marry her passion to her profession. This meant she had to take up creative designing as her main profession. Initially, she was apprehensive about whether she could succeed. But, I convinced her and the rest you already know. Today, she is one of the most sought after professionals in her field. And most importantly," Harry added, "she is enjoying her life like never before. There is a different glow on her face now."

"Can you please tell me how can I identify what my passion is?" Ryan, a young college student asked.

"Yes, yes!" Harry readily agreed, "but that will require some self-analysis."

"I am ready."

"All right then. Answer these questions.

- If you had all the time in the world
- If money was not a concern
- And, it really didn't matter what people said,

Then what professional activity would you choose?

"Please remember that it should be something that really excites you. If you immerse yourself in that activity, you will lose track of time. Even if someone wakes you in the middle of the night, you would be ready to do it."

Ryan was deep in thought. Harry asked all of us to do this exercise. After a couple of minutes, the boy suddenly said, "Technology! Anything to do with technology really excites me."

"And what makes you think so?" Harry asked gently.

"Ever since I was a child, electronic gadgets have fascinated me. Whenever my father brought me a new gadget, I would disassemble it, look at each part and assemble it properly and carefully. I even have a blog where I give my readers updates on the latest gizmos."

"Hmm, I think you have figured it out. Congratulations!"

Harry said, "Not many people succeed in the first attempt."

"Sir, but what if our passion is something that is commercially unviable?" a girl called Ayesha asked.

"Nothing in the world is commercially unviable," Harry replied instantly, "if you marry your passion to your profession, you will be able to generate wealth in many different ways.

"About six months back, I met Dr. Chang who is a renowned naturalist. He told me that human beings are the only species that worry about resources and make arrangements for the future. Animals never do. You will never find a goat saving bales of grass to meet future needs, or a rabbit accumulating as many carrots as possible to meet contingencies. They trust nature to provide them with their meals on a daily basis and interestingly, they get it every day! Surprisingly, whilst one fourth of humanity is perpetually malnourished, the percentage of animals who die out of hunger is relatively very low."

"But ants do collect food in the summer to meet their requirement in winter," Ayesha argued.

"Yes, but that is for that particular winter only. You will not find them accumulating resources for 10 years or 20 years, like we do!"

"Valid point!" she grinned.

"What I am trying to say is," Harry summed up, *"If you are aligned to your natural desires, then you don't have to worry about the resources. Nature will materialise for you whatever you want, whenever you want it."*

Harry showed us a video clip from a Bollywood movie, *Om Shanti Om*, and joked that the movie had not been sponsored by Om Group! Since I was not fluent in Hindi, Abhi translated the dialogues for me. In one scene, Shah Rukh Khan, the lead actor, said, *'Itni shiddat se maine tumhe paane ki koshish ki hai, ki har zarre ne mujhe tumse milaane ki saazish ki hai'*. This was the perfect example of what Harry was trying to tell us, when one had a burning desire to achieve something, then the Universe conspires in every way possible so that it can be achieved.

And then the actor said, *'Agar kisi cheez ko poore dil se chaho, to saari kaaynaat tumhe use milaane ki koshish mein lag jaati hai'*, which meant that if you loved something with all your heart, then the whole Universe would work hard towards making you achieve your dreams.

"Does that mean we can also attract things apart from money?" I asked Harry.

"Yes Dave," he said, "money is just a metaphor. When you follow your passion, or in other words, when your actions are motivated by the power of love, you can fulfil all your dreams."

"If that is true," I said, "then it is indeed miraculous."

"It is not miraculous, Dave. It is our birthright. It is every human being's right to fulfil all his dreams."

"Then why do so many dreams remain unfulfilled?"

"There can be two reasons for that. First, because most people are not following what their heart tells them to do. And second, sometimes we are not given what we want because something better is in store for us in the future!"

Harry refused to entertain further questions as he had started feeling dizzy.

"I will wind up today's session by giving you a 'dream manifestation technique'. With the help of this technique you can not only materialise money but anything else that you want. The only condition is you must have faith."

Harry explained that if someone's monthly income was Rs. 30,000 and if he asked the Universe to give him a Mercedes within a year, then he himself would have no faith in the feasibility of that request, and hence this wouldn't succeed.

It was not a question of being rational or irrational; it was just a question of generating enough faith to make the technique work powerfully. When Dhirubhai was a petrol pump attendant, he dreamt of owning the world's largest petroleum refinery. His friends and colleagues considered his ambitions irrational, but Dhirubhai could generate enough faith to make the technique work for him. Thus, it was natural faith and not logic that made the dream manifestation technique work.

"The technique involves three steps as shown here," he said while clicking for a new slide.

CHERISHED DREAMS + CONGRUENT ACTIONS + GOING WITH THE FLOW

"Let us discuss them one by one. The first step is to have Cherished Dreams. When I say cherished dreams," Harry clarified, "I mean dreams that really get you excited. They are in tune with your 'natural instincts'. So if you are pursuing a desire just to please your boss, or because your spouse wants you to do it, then the dream manifestation technique won't work. Someone has correctly said, *'There are two types of dreams. Those that you get after you fall asleep in the night, and those that give you sleepless nights!'*

"Here we are talking about those dreams that give you sleepless nights. Merely expecting or hoping for something does not qualify as a Cherished Dream.

"When he was a petrol pump attendant, Dhirubhai used to spend a long time looking at the gigantic Burmah Shell refinery and silently whispering to himself, 'One day, I shall own a similar refinery'. 'At times, I would sit there for hours,' Dhirubhai once told me, 'constantly looking at the refinery and closing my eyes, till it made a deep impression on my mind. It was then that my elder brother Ramanik would come out looking for me. Ramanik never had problem finding me, because he knew that I would be sitting on the pavement and dreaming. My friends thought I was crazy. But, when I used to sit there and dream, all thoughts of impossibilities would vanish. For a second, I would forget my current reality and would be totally absorbed by the thought of owning a refinery. My body would respond by giving me a 'Wow signal'.

"The Wow Signal is very critical," Harry said, "just close your eyes and concentrate on your body when you are thinking of your dream. If you get a 'Wow Signal', then it is confirmed that it is a Cherished Dream.

"You may have one dream or many. Some people even choose to make a goal chart where they write down all their goals and even stick pictures of them. Pictures help a great deal because that is the language your brain understands. Stick the chart in a prominent place in your room and frequently visualise your dreams coming true.

"There is a man in USA called John Goddard. When he was 15, he decided that he wanted to accomplish some extraordinary feats in his life. He took a piece of paper and wrote 127 dream tasks and called the list 'My Life List'. These were not easy or simple tasks. Some of them included exploring eight rivers, studying 12 primitive tribes, climbing 15 tall mountain peaks, visiting the best monuments in every country of the world,

circumnavigating the globe, reading the entire
Encyclopaedia Britannica, running a mile in five minutes,
learning French, Spanish, and Arabic, playing the flute and
violin, typing 50 words a minute, and many others.

"John placed his Life List on his drawing table. Every day
he would visualise his goals and gain inspiration from
them. But, unlike most people who have a habit of
forgetting their resolutions, John was determined to
accomplish his dreams.

"As unimaginable as it may sound," Harry said, while
reading from a paper, "John has already accomplished 109
of his super human quests. He was the first man in history
to explore the entire length of the Nile and Congo rivers.
He has also achieved the speed record of 1,500 mph in the
F-111 Fighter-Bomber, and an altitude record of 63,000
feet in the F-106 Delta Dart. In addition, he has climbed
12 of the world's highest mountains, conducted 14 major
expeditions into remote regions, traversed 15 of the
world's most treacherous rivers, visited 120 countries,
studied 260 primitive tribes, and travelled one million
miles during his adventurous life.

"The Los Angeles Times has called his expeditions one of the
most amazing adventures of this generation. But, what is
more intriguing is the support that John has got from
nature, because of his deep faith about his dreams. John
says that he never has had to worry about money. Wherever
he went, he met the right people who went out of their

way to support him. John has been bitten by a poisonous rattle snake, nearly chased to death by an elephant, been trapped in quicksand, crashed in planes, caught in an earthquake, and almost drowned twice in running rapids. Despite living on the edge, John has survived every single calamity and emerged victorious."

Harry showed us a book, *The Survivor* written by Goddard. The sub-title read, *24 Spine-Chilling Adventures on the Edge of Death*. He said that we should prepare our own goal charts by writing in clear words what we wanted. As per the rules defining quantum physics, the basic building block of matter was created when we paid 'attention to a certain thing'. The same applied to our goals. Whatever we pay attention to, will materialise. So if we want to look thin, we should write 'I want to look thin' instead of writing 'I don't want to look fat'. The language must be assertive, and not negative.

"The second step is to take congruent actions. By congruent actions I mean your actions must be consistent with the dreams that you want to achieve. If you heart urges you to become an astronaut, you can't take up a career in education. Once you assign your dream to nature, it will create events, coincidences, and circumstances in your life that take you closer to your goal. At such times, your only motive should be to capture every opportunity that will help you in fulfilling your dream.

"Every single action that you take must be absolutely in

sync with what you want. When Dhirubhai realised that his mediocre income was not enough to pursue his ambitions, he decided to speculate in the commodities market. The problem was that he had neither the knowledge nor contacts. So he approached a trader and expressed his desire to work for him. The trader refused saying that he already had enough employees. To this, Dhirubhai said that he was willing to work for free just to gain knowledge about the market.

"'The trader was shocked on hearing my words,' Dhirubhai laughed. 'He had never met anyone who would work for free, but such was my commitment to my goal. In the morning, I would go for my regular job, because I needed the salary, and in the evening I would work extra hours to gain knowledge'.

"And whether they were his struggling days in Yemen or his days of glory in India, Dhirubhai always displayed 100 percent commitment for his goals. 'Every day I worked hard to raise the bar for my company,' Dhirubhai told me, 'I don't visit art galleries, golf clubs, and horse races just because rich people are supposed to. I have never attended a film promotion, or cut a ribbon during any function. People have offered me the Director's position in various prestigious institutions, but I have politely declined them all. The whole corporate world has a 60-minute lunch break, but I finish my lunch in 20 minutes, because lunch is just a compulsion, the real passion lies in spending time in creating something big!' he would say.

"So the second and a very crucial step in the dream manifestation technique is congruent actions," Harry reiterated. "If you want to cut down belly fat, you have to avoid the chocolate pastries. I know it's very difficult for some people to resist high calorie food, but if looking thin is a cherished dream, then you will be able to control the temptation, not otherwise.

"And the third and the last step is, 'Go with the flow'.

"When you assign your dreams to nature it will work towards fulfilling it. Some dreams may be fulfilled instantly, some may take few days, some may take many years. Whatever may be the case, when I say 'go with the flow' I mean not resisting whatever is happening and allowing it to happen.

"Once you plant a seed in the ground, do you dig it again and again to check how it is growing? No. You simply plant the seed and leave it to nature. When will the seed sprout? When will the shoots appear? When will the leaves emerge? These are not our concerns. Quite similarly, once you have assigned your dreams to nature, it is its duty to fulfil it for you. How it does this, and what approach it uses, should not be worried about.

"When Dhirubhai nurtured the dream to own a big petroleum refinery, he didn't get it straightaway. Instead, he had to start from the very opposite end of what he wanted. First, he ventured into textiles. Then he moved one step backwards and started producing the polyester that goes into the making of textiles. Then, he moved one more step backwards and started making the polymer intermediaries that make polyester. Next, he went further back and started making petroleum products. And ultimately, he took the last step back and created the petroleum refinery that he had always dreamt of.

"Ultimately, his dream was achieved. But by not fulfilling it straightaway and taking him through a reverse route; nature not only gave him what he wanted, but also helped him create one of the world's biggest corporate empires.

"That's how the game of life works," Harry said, "Sometimes life says 'yes' and gives us what we want. Sometimes it says 'no', and gives us something better and sometimes it says 'wait' and gives us the best!"

Harry advised that we must never fret over a broken relationship, or a failed venture. When life takes something away from us, it is not punishing us. It is merely emptying our hands, so that we can receive something better.

"So with this we complete the 'dream manifestation' technique and the Third Secret Law of Money. I have some good news for you," he paused and waited till all of us were straining to hear him tell us what it was. "Saloni has organised a party for all of you after lunch. First, I will talk to you for a little while more, and then you can enjoy the songs selected for you by the DJ."

"Yoooo!" we all screamed ecstatically.

"But, before I wind up for today, I want to tell you a story which is one of my favourites.

"Once upon a time, a father took his son to a revered spiritual guru. He complained that his son was deeply interested in pursuing a career in music, but he wanted him to pursue a career in agriculture.

'Please guide him, master,' the father pleaded, 'for many months I have been trying to convince him that by pursuing agriculture, he can earn more money for the family, but he just doesn't listen. All he does is fiddle with his musical instruments the whole day long.'

The master did not say anything but requested the father to meet him the next day.

And the father did as he was told, and reached the monastery early next morning. He looked everywhere but couldn't find the master. Finally, as he was about to leave, he saw the master standing in one corner of the garden outside the monastery. He seemed to be in a really bad temper.

'I want you to be roses! Do you understand?' he was screaming to a fresh lily blossom. 'I want you to be roses!'

And then turning to the father he said, 'You see these idiots!' he pointed to the lilies, 'For so many days I have been telling them to be roses. But they just don't seem to listen!'

'But why do you want roses?'

'Because roses will get me more money.'

'But how can you expect a lily plant to bear roses?'

'The same way you expect a musician to become a farmer!' the master chuckled.

"The father instantly understood. From that day onwards, he stopped nagging at his son and instead focused on nurturing his innate talent. And, legend says, that little boy became one of the greatest musicians that the country had produced!

"Remember," Harry told us, "Nature believes in uniqueness. No two natural creations are identical. Pluck a leaf from a tree, you will not find any other leaf in this world that is identical to it. No two flakes of snow that ever fell on this planet are identical. As human beings, we know that each one of us has a different voice and a different set of fingerprints, but it is equally true that each one of us has a unique 'skill set' which no one has.

"The reason why nature is so beautiful and ever-rejoicing is because everything in nature is in harmony with itself. A lily plant does not try to give roses, and a grapevine does not struggle to grow as tall as the palm tree. The moment you identify your naturally bestowed skills and start working on it, all your actions will be in harmony with yourself. And then success, money, fame, and happiness will automatically follow!

"This is my last message to you!"

———

FIND A JOB YOU LOVE AND YOU WILL NEVER WORK A DAY IN YOUR LIFE
—CONFUCIUS

During the lunch break, we had the privilege of sharing a table with Harry. He was still under medication and the doctors had advised him to have a very simple meal. We were leaving for Mumbai that very night and were listening to his final instructions.

"Here you are," he said handing over a stack of papers to Abhi, "these are the companies who are interesting in conducting this course for their staff. Please coordinate with them."

"And Dave," he said, turning to me, "You start finalising your manuscript. I want it to be published as soon as possible. We already have a sizeable number of orders."

Harry told us that he had assigned these tasks, based on our passions. Abhi had a flair for training, and I had a flair for writing. Since we would be doing what we loved to do, it was going to be fun!

Our conversation was interrupted by Saloni walking in with a thick bag, full of books, and DVDs.

"What's this?" Abhi asked.

"It's a collection of rare motivational books and videos, which you both will find useful. I don't need it anymore, so you can use it for your reference," Harry said, smiling at the shock on our faces.

"That's a lot of material!" I exclaimed.

"You see, when passion meets profession, a lot can be materialised!" Harry chuckled.

We had a hearty laugh together.

5

PASSING THE TORCH

After lunch, we all met again, in the training hall, dressed in our formal clothes for the valedictory ceremony. Both Abhi and I were feeling sad about reaching the end of an event that had transformed our lives. We wanted to stay back forever and yet, we wanted to start off on our new goals as well. Each morning we had spent here was so inspiring and gave us a lot of energy. And how could we forget Harry? Although the others had become attached to him as well, we had had the privilege of sharing a personal bond with him.

"It may be over for them Dave," Abhi said as we too occupied our seats, "but for us it is just the beginning."

"Yes," I agreed. "A lot of work and a great responsibility."

"Responsibility can be a burden or a privilege. It depends on how you look at it," he pointed out.

Yeah! Yeah! I felt like telling him, 'Don't flaunt your

ontological knowledge in front of me', but Abhi was suddenly busy staring at Saloni who was looking stunningly gorgeous in a black dress.

"A female can be a burden or a privilege," I giggled. "It depends on how you look at it!"

"Shuddup!" he pounced on me, embarrassed that I had noticed.

Thankfully, Harry entered the hall at that very moment and Abhi was forced to stop pummelling me!

A jubilant audience greeted Harry with wild applause.

"Unbelievable!" he exclaimed. "On the first day we met, half of you were sleeping and the other half were bored to death. But judging by the way you welcomed me, I can conveniently presume that you had a great time during the course."

"Yo!" we all cheered.

"Well, then, I have already told you whatever I intended to," he flapped through the pages of the secret diary glancing at every page. "The tools that I have given you will help you fulfil all your dreams, achieve success, and most importantly create abundant wealth.

"One of the participants from my previous courses once asked me if I strongly believed that if there is no free lunch, why do I give free training sessions?

"And I must admit that it was an excellent question. Only a person who has listened to me attentively could ask me that. In fact, what he suggested is correct in a certain context. The Payback Theory says that you must give some sort of gurudakshina or energy exchange to any person who gives you knowledge. But, the new ideology suggests that instead of paying back it is better to 'Pay Forward'. If someone gives you knowledge and you pay back with money, then the circle is complete. There is no further development. But instead of paying back, if you pay forward by sharing the knowledge with someone else, and he too pays it forward then the chain will continue till eternity. So the course is not free, there is a price tag attached. And the price is that you will pass it forward to others.

"If I was in the Second School of Vedic life, I would have asked you to payback. As a householder, money is a must. But now I am in the third phase of my life, and since I have retired, seeking wealth is not a priority. I have already built my pipelines. Now, I want to do something for society, and hence I insist on paying forward so that we can continue this chain and impact more and more people."

Harry told us a story. An old man was planting a tree when a young boy came and asked him, 'You will not live long to eat the fruits of this tree, then why are you planting it?' And the man replied, 'I am not planting these seeds for myself. They are for you, my son. When you grow up you will enjoy the fruits of this tree. And when you become old, you too must plant some seeds, so that your children may enjoy the fruits.'

"Over the last few days I have shared with you some very powerful secrets from my experience," he waved the secret diary. "Dhirubhai too desired that more and more people be inspired by his rags-to-riches story and achieve phenomenal success. Although there is no compulsion, I urge you to pay forward, by sharing these techniques with people around you. Be it your family, your neighbours, friends, relatives, colleagues, clients, members in your community, and others. And the more you give, the more will come back to you. The mysterious law always works. *When you share this knowledge from your heart, without any grudges or resistance, it creates positive karma, and whatever you have shared will multiply and come back to you.* When you make a difference in people's lives, it gives you a sort of divine joy which can never be expressed in words.

"When I was about 12 years old, my father told me of Mahatma Gandhi's Dandi March. He explained how the British had imposed tax on salt, which was a necessary commodity. A majority of Indians were poor and couldn't afford this extra burden. Gandhiji felt it was unjust. To voice his protest, he walked from Ahmedabad to a place called Dandi, traversing a distance of 240 miles, a landmark journey that lasted 24 days. On reaching Dandi, he took a pinch of salt in his hand and declared civil disobedience against the British rule.

"I was impressed with the story. But, I couldn't understand one thing. 'Why did he walk so much?' I asked my father. 'Why did he walk for 240 miles and waste 24 days? He could have simply taken a train and reached there in a single day.'

"My father laughed at my naïve question. But he gave me an answer that really left me thinking for a long time. 'The Dandi march wasn't about protesting the salt law alone,' he explained. 'The protest was undoubtedly real, but the bigger intention was to create an awakening amongst millions of Indians and enroll them in the freedom struggle. During the day Gandhiji would walk for about ten miles and in the evening he would talk to the villagers and urge them to join his mission. As he passed any village, thousands of people were inspired by his words and joined him in the march. Millions of others keenly followed this movement through the news relayed by the papers and the radio. All leading newspapers of the world carried reports and pictures of his march every day. When he left Ahmedabad, Gandhiji had only a handful of followers, but by the time he reached Dandi 60,000 people had joined the march and millions broke the law in their own way in different parts of the country. Had Gandhiji travelled in a train,' my father reasoned, 'he would have reached Dandi in one day, but wouldn't have succeeded in enrolling the people and spreading his message.'

Harry told us that enrolment was the best way of propagating a message. All great leaders — Prophet Muhammad, Karl Marx, Buddha, Martin Luther, and many others — used it to take their message to the masses. Initially, the concept of non-violence was Gandhiji's personal philosophy. Only he believed in it. But as an individual it would have been tough to fight the British. So Gandhi 'enrolled' more and more people for his cause and created a force which helped him strengthen his purpose. With the combined strength of millions of satyagrahis, he shook the foundation of the British Empire.

"Last Christmas, I was struck in a traffic jam in Mumbai. There was nothing much I could do in a car and hence thought of wishing a couple of friends a 'Merry Christmas'. One of them is based in New York, and the other stays in Sydney. Perchance during the conversation they too mentioned that they were struck in a traffic jam. For a second, I was shocked, how can three people in three different cities face the same problem at the same time? And the very next minute the answer hit me, almost like a thunderbolt! It was Jesus Christ! All over the world people were celebrating his birthday.

"What an amazing life that man must have lived," Harry's face lit up. "Two thousand years after his birth, he could cause traffic jams almost all over the world! This is perhaps the greatest example of enrolment. Christ lived for only 33 years, but by enrolling people for his cause, he gave immortality to his message.

"Out there in the world there are billions of people living in poverty. Even amongst them those who are well off earn money only after tremendous struggles. A certain percentage of them might be victims of circumstance, but a majority of them are responsible for their own fate. They are so hellbent on maintaining their cheap beliefs and lazy lifestyles that it isn't surprising that they are suffering. Bill Gates once said, 'If you are born poor, it isn't your fault. But if you die poor, it certainly is.'

"We are not here to criticise them," Harry said. "Instead, my only request to you would be that you enrol such people, give them this knowledge and ask them to pay it forward. Till date we have only helped people with resources, but resources without 'financial literacy' are futile. The Chinese have a proverb, 'Teach a man to fish, he eats today. Teach him how to fish – he eats every day.'

"When the earthquake hit Saroon, we only gave resources to the locals. But, it was only a temporary solution. Then I decided to 'gift' the locals this course, and it produced miracles. The first course here had only 12 participants. After witnessing the impact the course had on their lives, 50 more people enrolled for the next course, and then 100 in the next. Month after month, the numbers were rising. We couldn't accommodate so many people, and so we shifted to this big auditorium. Even the frequency of the sessions has increased, but it doesn't help. Currently, we have courses lined up back to back and yet there is a two-month waiting period for those who want to participate. Even if I train people for the rest of my life I will hardly be able to impact a miniscule population. And so I have decided to use the power of enrolment. Dhirubhai enrolled me, I enrolled you and you will enrol others. The other day I told you about the magical power of Replication'. Enrolment, too, is a form of replication, albeit for a more noble cause.

"I once read a proverb — 'A pebble tossed in a pond touches the water at a single point, but the ripples it creates affects the whole pond.' We may not live for long, but the transformation that our actions will bring, will live till eternity."

As always, Harry ended the session with an inspirational story.

"Have you ever seen a mother sparrow teaching its little one to fly? It takes its baby to the edge of the tree's branch and urges it to jump. The baby is afraid of falling down, and hence it resists. Since birth it has only used its legs. It has no idea what it is like to fly with its wings. But its mother knows that *using its wings are its inherent nature. They just have to be flapped to reach out to the skies*'. So, suddenly, the mother gives the baby a final push from the branch. The baby sparrow falls down immediately, but just when it is about to hit the ground, its wings take over instinctively and it takes off towards the skies. And from then onwards, it flies for the rest of its life.

"Quite similarly, when people come to my course they come with gigantic dreams. Be it the sales executive of Om Group, or a local grain dealer. But they are afraid of falling down and hence resist the take-off. My job is to push you, because I know that dreams are your inherent nature. They just have to be expressed and you too can reach out to the skies!"

And that day, quite spontaneously, all the participants stood up and their standing ovation for Mr. Haribhai Shah was testimony to the immense gratitude they felt.

He had touched the deepest core of our heart.

The powerful secrets that Harry shared with Abhi and Dave at Saroon are now available in an exciting new multimedia kit. Discover rare secrets (some of which are not mentioned in this book) on fulfilling your dreams, creating massive wealth and achieving success.

For more information log on to www.saroonsecrets.com

Dear Reader,

We hope you have enjoyed reading this book. If you wish to be associated with us and receive updates on our books, DVDs, trainings, newsletters etc., kindly please fill the form below and send it to : **Dhaval Bathia, Genesis Education, Ground Floor, Haridwar Building, Mathuradas Road, Kandivali (W), Mumbai 400 067, INDIA. Alternatively, you may also send a mail to** dhavalbathia@yahoo.com

Name: _____

Address: _____

_____

E-mail: _____

Company/Institution: _____

Designation: _____ Phone:_____

Feedback (about this book) _____

_____

_____

_____

_____

_____

Any other queries/comments: _____

_____

_____

_____

JAICO PUBLISHING HOUSE
Elevate Your Life. Transform Your World.

Established in 1946, Jaico Publishing House is the publisher of stellar authors such as Sri Sri Paramahansa Yogananda, Osho, Robin Sharma, Deepak Chopra, Stephen Hawking, Eknath Easwaran, Sarvapalli Radhakrishnan, Nirad Chaudhuri, Khushwant Singh, Mulk Raj Anand, John Maxwell, Ken Blanchard and Brian Tracy. Our list which has crossed a landmark 2000 titles, is amongst the most diverse in the country, with books in religion, spirituality, mind/body/spirit, self-help, business, cookery, humour, career, games, biographies, fiction, and science.

Jaico has expanded its horizons to become a leading publisher of educational and professional books in management and engineering. Our college-level textbooks and reference titles are used by students countrywide. The success of our academic and professional titles is largely due to the efforts of our Educational and Corporate Sales Divisions.

The late Mr. Jaman Shah established Jaico as a book distribution company. Sensing that independence was around the corner, he aptly named his company Jaico ("Jai" means victory in Hindi). In order to tap the significant demand for affordable books in a developing nation, Mr. Shah initiated Jaico's own publications. Jaico was India's first publisher of paperback books in the English language.

In addition to being a publisher and distributor of its own titles, Jaico is a major distributor of books of leading international publishers such as McGraw Hill, Pearson, Cengage Learning, John Wiley and Elsevier Science. With its headquarters in Mumbai, Jaico has other sales offices in Ahmedabad, Bangalore, Bhopal, Chennai, Delhi, Hyderabad and Kolkata. Our sales team of over 40 executives, direct mail order division, and website ensure that our books effectively reach all urban and rural parts of the country.

SINCE 1946